Bryan & h

C000060747

Exhibitionism

Best wishes

Chris.

Exhibitionism

A Popular History of Performance and Display

Chris Nancollas

DARTON·LONGMAN+TODD

First published in 2013 by
Darton, Longman and Todd Ltd
1 Spencer Court
140 – 142 Wandsworth High Street
London SW18 4JJ

© 2013 Chris Nancollas

The right of Chris Nancollas to be identified as the Author of this
work has been asserted in accordance with the Copyright, Designs
and Patents Act 1988.

ISBN 978-0-232-52915-9

A catalogue record for this book is available from the British Library.

Thanks are due to Faber and Faber for permission to reproduce lines
from 'Annus Mirabilis' taken from *Collected Poems* by Philip Larkin
(Faber and Faber, 1988).

Phototypeset by Kerrypress Ltd, Luton, Bedfordshire
Printed and bound by Bell & Bain, Glasgow

Contents

Acknowledgements

Sarah Draisey tracked down numerous obscure interviews with comedians, which was a great help in the performance section of the book.

Just as I was finishing this book, I was diagnosed with a rare form of chronic leukaemia. Fortunately, it has been successfully treated, but it did mean that the final launch was delayed. I would like to thank all of the staff at DLT, and especially Will Parkes, for their support during this difficult period.

Most of all, though, I would like to thank my wife Sue, who not only had to put up with an author, but a sick one at that. My recovery is due in large part to her care and attention. I would also like to thank my wider family and friends for their support and encouragement. It means a lot when the chips are down.

Finally, my survival is due to the excellent care I received at Gloucester Royal and Cheltenham General Hospitals. The NHS is getting a battering these days, but I have nothing but praise for the way I was treated.

1

Introduction

This book is all about mankind's need to make an exhibition of himself – or, as we shall see, herself. The origins of the human need for public display are lost in the mists of time, but exhibitionism of one sort or another has flourished throughout mankind's history. And it appears that what we call exhibitionism, the display of the male genitalia, began at the very dawn of civilisation. The earliest known cave paintings feature representations of penile display and actual models of the penis, as well as voluptuous female drawings and figurines. As mankind lives longer and inhabits more complex societies, then public nudity diminishes, and slowly gains an aura of shame. Religion and the relatively new science of psychiatry reinforce that view, placing exhibitionism firmly as a sin or a sexual deviation respectively.

Until, that is, the late twentieth century. The public opinion of exhibitionism has shifted dramatically in the last fifty years, reflecting the changing values of modern society. Although genital exhibition by lone males is still considered abnormal, the cultural changes of the postmodern era have legitimised some forms of nudity which were previously thought to be taboo. For example, magazines featuring topless women were not on general sale even as recently as the 1950s, but by the 1970s a best-selling newspaper, *The Sun*, had its 'Page 3 girls'– an idea quickly copied by other tabloid newspapers. Full frontal nudity in top shelf magazines came shortly afterwards, while the naked human form moved out of the strip clubs and onto the stage in the musicals *Hair* and *Oh! Calcutta!* For a while, there was a strange dichotomy between male nudity and female – the female form was considered titillating, while the male was obscene. But now the male stripper is as ubiquitous as the female, and exhibitionism has come out of the closet.

Unfortunately, that closet has the word 'pervert' stamped over the door, and means that the word 'exhibitionism' is primarily linked with the sexual disorder. There are, in fact, two definitions; the first is a psychosexual disorder characterised by the exposure of the genitalia to strangers, and the second a tendency towards display or exaggerated behaviour of any kind.

Genital exhibitionism is a paraphilia, a disorder of normal sexual function, and closely linked to voyeurism and other sex aberrations. The paraphilias are often considered humorous and relatively harmless, but they can be a front for much more severe psychosexual, and psychiatric, problems. The psychology of sexual deviancy is a labyrinth of related delinquencies, some of which are anything but laughable or harmless.

The second definition of an exhibitionist is a person who takes part in an exhibition or public performance, or is prone to flamboyant behaviour. So exhibitionists are not just drooling flashers wandering round in their plastic macs, but also people who engage in public display, especially those who give exaggerated performances – the shock artist, the ham actor, or the over-the-top comedian.

This second definition will form the other part of our study. By its very nature, art – be it painting, sculpture, acting or music – requires a degree of exhibitionism, the need to display one's self or one's work. Artists must have a certain psychological makeup to be able to function, the artistic courage to put their work before the public expecting it to be judged. To anyone trying to analyse the career of artists, this is the one thing that stands out – their ability to get known, get published, or get the part in the film. The successful artist has, somewhere, the ruthlessness to exploit his or her work for commercial gain – the exhibitionist gene, if you like. Every successful artist or band sits on a pyramid of thousands of others who don't make it, even if they are just as talented in the technical aspects of their craft. They either lack the courage to take that final step and submit their work to public display, or they reject the inevitable compromises which accompany collective endeavour. And others have only a fraction of the talent, but possess a genius for publicity. The world of the arts is full of stories about the ruthlessness, and luck, of some artists and how they have managed to achieve the summit of their profession with apparently minimal ability. Although I have no doubt that there is an element of sour grapes here – the truest line ever spoken in a film was, 'I could have been a contender', famously uttered by Marlon Brando in Elia Kazan's 1954 masterpiece *On the Waterfront*. I bet we can all think of people who have risen to the top of the tree not just through talent, but also by a combination of flattery, backstabbing, and general ruthlessness. The career path for the famous is almost Darwinian in its composition. Even artists who are renowned for being reclusive – one thinks of the poet R. S. Thomas, or the author Cormac McCarthy – have crossed that initial line and got their work into the public domain.

There are two avenues to explore in artistic exhibition, the generic psychology of the artist, and the psychology of those on the edge, the exhibitionists within the exhibitionists. The second half of the twentieth century saw the growth of new forms of art, in all its disciplines, some of which stretch the boundaries of art in ways which more conventional artists see as heretical. In some of these works it is the name of the artist that is as important as the work itself. The world of the arts has always had its share of rampant egos, but the last fifty years have seen the cult of personality equal, and sometimes eclipse, the artistic merit of the work on offer.

To give you an example, take the Beatles. I was ten when they released 'She Loves You'. It was a piece of classic pop music, and though the band supplemented their genius with good looks and charm, what happened next was phenomenal. Their name spread like wildfire, even down to no-radio-reception rural Cornwall where I lived. Teenage girls screamed incessantly through their concerts and fought through the mass ranks of security simply to touch them. Fuelled by the rise of the broadcast media, they went from relative unknowns to near deities (and I mean that quite literally) in a disturbingly short period of time. By 1964 and the release of 'A Hard Day's Night', they could have recorded the national anthem and it would have got to number one. It was the artist, as well the art, which was important; something that has always been there but took flight in the second half of the twentieth century.

Another form of public display that could be considered exhibitionist is architecture. At first I worried this was stretching the definition too far, but in the course of my research I came to believe that this was perhaps the most important branch of public display. Most of the population would struggle to remember a Roman poet, a Roman law, or even more than two or three Roman emperors, but they know about the Coliseum or Hadrian's Wall. Buildings designed beyond the mere functional are exhibitions of skill, power, and wealth, and what is great architecture if it not exhibitionism in its most enduring form?

There is one final avenue which this book will explore, and this goes back to genital display. The rise of the internet has seen a huge increase in the number of people with access to pornography, which has itself become one of the most popular subjects on the net. This has resulted in something almost unthinkable even twenty years ago – the open discussion of pornography by users, who now include women. This in turn has led to the legitimisation of the porn industry, especially in the USA, where they even have award ceremonies equivalent to the Oscars. (No prizes for guessing what the statuettes are shaped like.) The actresses are famous and the industry is seen by some as a legitimate, even admirable, way of getting on in the world. So what is happening here? The ultimate form of exhibitionism, having sex in public, previously considered to be unmentionable, is now acceptable or nearly respectable, at least in some quarters.

So this book is not just about genital exposure, but public display and exhibitionism in all its forms: sex, art, the performing arts, and architecture. But first, we have to go back to prehistory, to the dank caves of the Palaeolithic Era, and find the earliest representation of the genitalia in human history. This is where the tale of exhibitionism begins, on the first page of the human story.

2

The history of exhibitionism

The oldest known depiction of a phallus was found in the Hohle Fels cave in Germany, and was not a picture but a model, life sized and cut from stone. In the same cave were found a female figurine, thought to depict Venus, and one of the earliest known musical instruments, a bone flute. These were made roughly 28,000 years ago, in the prehistoric Upper Palaeolithic period, and are among the oldest human artefacts in existence. This era sees the emergence of human figurines, notably Venus representations of the female form, which have given rise to much speculation as to the nature of Upper Palaeolithic society. Some see the profusion of female forms as evidence of a matriarchal society, others thought they were a fertility symbol, and one historian wondered if they represented a form of pornography. The stone phallus has been mooted as an early sex aid, although that is obviously a matter of conjecture. As the tools of the Old Stone Age were fairly primitive, the stone phallus would have taken quite a bit of work – an indication perhaps of its importance to mankind's earliest ancestors.

The Upper Palaeolithic period also saw the creation of figurative art in the cave paintings of France and Spain. The most famous are in Lascaux in southern France, the paintings depicting hunting scenes and featuring bison and bulls.

The discovery of Lascaux in 1940 stimulated the search for more sites, and cave paintings have now been found on all four major continents. One of the most interesting finds was in the cave of Los Casares in Spain, which had recognisable depictions of the male phallus and the sex act. Other images have been found which look like masturbation and oral sex, and some of the images depict a third figure apparently observing the sex act. The latter is most likely thought to be a shamanic presence rather than the world's first voyeur, although opinions vary. What seems to be clear is that as mankind evolved, social and sexual behaviour became more complex and public display became part of society.

It would be wrong to suggest that sexual imagery was prehistoric man's overriding concern. Judging by the number of images so far discovered, the Neanderthal artist's main inspiration was the depiction of animals, either as part of a hunt or just for plain decoration. The profusion of animal remains from the period led one historian to describe Palaeolithic Europe as, 'a human desert swarming with game,' so it appears that our hunting forebears were just making a faithful record of their environment. But that in itself is significant, because painting is a form of public display, indicating that from the earliest times exhibiting skill has been important to human beings.

Cave painting and the fashioning of Venus figurines continue into the Neolithic period, where slowly the modern society takes shape. Primitive communities evolve as our ancestors move from the cave to the village. Tools become more complex, grain is cultivated, clothing is fashioned, and hunting weaponry becomes more sophisticated as the arrow and the spear become easier to produce. The earliest pottery appears. As the ability to produce more food increases, humans become healthier and live longer. The historian J. M. Roberts, in his book *The History of the World*, believes the rate of human progress was directly related to the size of the population – in other words, the more numerous a gathering, the more ideas were generated and the faster that society developed.

There is also evidence of conflict, with an increase in the number of skeletons displaying trauma, the nature of which indicated that they were inflicted by weapons. As the Neolithic Era gives way to the Bronze Age, technology becomes more sophisticated, with the sword and the plough appearing. In Britain, the Neolithic peoples began the first monument at Stonehenge, indicating that ritual and display were becoming increasingly refined. The famous stones were erected later, in the Bronze Age, and additions to the monument were made right through to the Iron Age. Whatever Stonehenge is, or was (and the speculation could last until the end of this book), the whole Stonehenge system of monuments, burials and procession routes indicates a society which was capable of sophisticated construction, precise measurement, and concerted collective effort. As they left no written records, just layers of mystery, we can only use informed archaeological speculation as to the nature of their society. Stonehenge is an exhibition of something, we just don't know exactly what it is.

The world's oldest recognised civilisation began in Mesopotamia, the Fertile Crescent between the Rivers Tigris and Euphrates, corresponding to modern-day Iran and Iraq. Here the world's first written symbols were discovered, characters inscribed on clay cylinders, recording lists of goods and receipts, stock levels and other simple trading memoranda. The initial motivation for the invention of writing appears to be practical, to record a surplus of goods and foodstuffs too great for the individual to remember. This simple pictorial record slowly developed into a form of writing, Sumerian cuneiform. This is one of the great human milestones; probably the single greatest achievement between the development of agriculture and the invention of the steam engine. It transformed all forms of human interaction, notably in commerce, and led directly to the development of a complex intellectual and artistic life.

One of the world's first stories is the Epic of Gilgamesh, a long saga in verse style, probably first written down about 200BC. The story centres on the friendship of Gilgamesh, the mighty king of Uruk (part man, part God), with a wild man called Enkidu, who the Gods have created to distract Gilgamesh from his oppression of the citizens of Uruk. They embark on a series of quests together, most of which incur the displeasure of the Gods, and are too complex to relate here. The story of Enkidu, though, is very interesting. He is created by the Gods out of clay and roams the Earth as a wild man, living with animals. He sets his animal friends free from traps, which causes one trapper to seek help from Gilgamesh. The trapper is instructed to take the harlot Shamhat to the water hole, where she is instructed to 'expose' herself to Enkidu and seduce him. This she does revealing her breasts and 'exposing her sex'. She, 'performed the task of womankind,' while 'his lust groaned over her.' After seven days (!) his wildness is tamed, the beasts run away from him and Shamhat brings him to Gilgamesh.

Genital exhibition is therefore a central component in of one of the earliest human stories. It is interesting that the world's first exhibitionist is a woman, Shamhat, and that she is described as a 'temple prostitute'. This indicates society has evolved well past the point where sex is used for procreation alone, and that recreational sex has become a fact. The appearance of a prostitute in the story confirms its status as 'the world's oldest profession', and it indicates that human relationships are already in stormy waters. And the effect of sex on Enkidu, which tames him and draws him into human society, is also extremely interesting from all sorts of angles. Is the 'task of womankind' – a phrase used at least twice in the epic – meant to indicate that women were responsible for civilising men? It is impossible to speculate, but it appears that the tables were turned at some point, because there are all sorts of rules in later Sumerian Society regarding adultery and the conditions necessary to justify stoning a woman to death. The creator of *Rumpole,* John Mortimer, often pointed out that if prostitution was the world's oldest profession, the second oldest was the law, and the profusion of legislation in Sumerian society would appear to back him up.

Aside from their legal systems, the Sumerians were the first people to depict the lifelike human form in art. Many of the images are of processions, showing clothed figures engaged in some form of ritual. There are carvings and statuettes of lifelike women both clothed and naked. Some are holding symbols, and they often appear surrounded by animals, especially owls. An intricate pantheology is emerging, which reflects the complexities of human evolution.

Ancient Sumeria declined and was succeeded by the Babylonian and Assyrian empires. This is not the place to dissect these empires in detail, but no book that deals with the story of human sexuality can pass by Babylon, the fabled city of antiquity, whose ruler Nebuchadnezzar besieged Jerusalem and enslaved the Israelites. More written tablets were found there than in any other Mesopotamian site, which means that we know more about Babylon than most other ancient cities. The texts unearthed indicated that the Babylonians had developed the old cuneiform writing, making it possible to record increasingly complex theoretical and practical activity. Astronomy was developed in Babylon, as was mathematics, and surviving tablets show an extensive knowledge of medicine and law.

The most famous list of laws dating from that time is the Code of Hammurabi, which contains nearly three hundred separate articles. They are quite comprehensive on the subject of stealing, fraud, violence, adultery and incest, and although men are just 'men' throughout, adult women are 'wives', 'prostitutes', or 'sisters of the God' (which may be a euphemism for harlot). 'Sisters of the God' are forbidden from owning – or even entering – taverns, presumably because of their effect on drunken men. And the goddess Ishtar, the Mesopotamian goddess of fertility, is also linked with prostitution, as the patroness of the temple prostitutes. All this would seem to indicate that illicit love, or at least adultery and consorting with prostitutes, was an accepted part of Babylonian life, and there were laws to deal with its manifestations. From this time on, most of the great cities and civilisations will have a similarly complex attitude to affairs of the heart. One suspects that lurking in the background of all this lechery are the paraphilias, like voyeurism and exhibitionism. It would go with the territory.

Although other cities were probably equally sordid as dens of iniquity, Babylon has attained infamy because of the Bible, mentioned in the book of Daniel in the Old Testament and the Book of Revelations, the final book of the New Testament. Daniel was a captive Israelite in the kingdom of Babylon, a seer, able to interpret the dreams of Nebuchadnezzar and his successor Belshazzar, and have prophetic dreams of his own. He interpreted the words of the 'moving finger' writing on the walls at Belshazzar's feast, which foretold the end of the Babylonian empire. (When it came, Daniel was famously thrown into the lion's den.) Belshazzar had worshipped false gods and his feasts became a byword for debauchery; a fitting climax for an evil society.

Revelations was the work of St John of Patmos, who was given the vision by an angel. The work is complex and full of symbolism, but is basically the story of the conquest of evil and the establishment of a New Jerusalem. Evil appears in the form of, 'a woman mounted on a scarlet beast which was covered with blasphemous names and had seven heads and ten horns'. And, 'on her forehead was a name written: MYSTERY, BABYLON THE GREAT, THE MOTHER OF HARLOTS AND ABOMINATIONS OF THE EARTH'. The 'kings of the earth have committed fornication with her, and the inhabitants of the earth have been made drunk with the wine of her fornication'. This quite clearly separates sexual activity into 'good', that is, 'normal' pro-creational sex, and 'bad' – prostitution, adultery and the various paraphilias and perversions. This image of Babylon as a centre of evil, 'the whore of Babylon,' has persisted to the present day, and is actively kept alive in one religion in particular. Not the Church of England – I expect if you asked a modern Church of England vicar about Revelations, he or she would probably pause and say: 'Moving swiftly on ... ' – but the Rastafarian religion. For the Rasta, Babylon is the rest of the world, and the great oppressing power of Western civilisation in particular. As it is the religion of working-class West Indians, especially Jamaicans, the oppressors are the colonial English. Rastafarians exhibit their religion in the form of dreadlocks and their characteristic red, yellow and black headgear. The important thing to remember is Babylon as a metaphor for all evil, and sexual evil, of which exhibitionism is a part.

The other great cradle of civilisation was Ancient Egypt, which developed from about 3000BC, roughly parallel with that of ancient Mesopotamia. From the point of view of exhibitionism, Egypt is important for two reasons. First, it left us with its curious deities. The Egyptian pantheon was extensive and to our modern minds quite strange; some of the gods having the heads of birds and animals – for example: Anubis, the god of the dead, has a jackal head; Horus, the god of the sky, a hawk's head; and Thoth, the god of writing, the head of an ibis.

Most of the gods are symbolic and some have sexual imagery. The dwarf god Bes, protector of pregnant women, is sometimes depicted with a phallus. As is Osiris, the god of the underworld, whose story is quite bizarre: he is killed and hacked to pieces by his brother Seth, the lord of chaos (another god with an animal head). Osiris is put together by his wife Isis, goddess of healing, and brought back to life, but with one important difference – Isis is unable to find his genitalia and has to fashion a new, larger, set of organs. This event was celebrated in a festival, with women parading the streets with giant phalluses. And it seems that genital exposure was practised as a fertility rite. During the festival for Bastet, the cat god, women would expose their genitalia, and exposure of female genitalia to statues of Apis, the bull, encouraged fertility. The god Min was depicted as a human with an erect penis. Some prostitutes were said to walk around nearly naked, covered only with tattoos. Nonetheless, gods aside, Egyptian sexual practices seem similar to our own, aside from the overt phallic imagery common to all ancient peoples.

We do not typically remember Ancient Egypt, however, for its sexuality, but the power and majesty of its buildings. The Pyramids; the Sphinx; the temples at Thebes and Luxor: these are not dwellings or storehouses but statements, powerful messages from a society rich enough and skilled enough to leave their imprint on the world. 'My name is Ozymandias, King of Kings, look on my works ye mighty and despair!' wrote Shelley, putting words into the mouth of Ozymandias, otherwise known as Ramesses the Great, who ruled in about 1200BC. The invader from the East may pass the borders with hope in his heart, but one look at the Pyramids and he would realise that the game was up. A society capable of such a wonder had to be all-powerful. And they buried their kings in golden sarcophagi surrounded by fabulous wealth, a rich display of earthly power.

Further afield, civilisation was also developing in India and China, although slightly later than Mesopotamian and Egyptian society. The Hindu god Shiva, one of the oldest Gods in the world, had a phallus as his emblem. Phallic imagery and female figurines have been found at Mohenjo-Daro, the oldest archaeological site in the Indus valley, dating from around 2,500BC.

We know less about ancient China, although some ancient bronze phallic objects have been unearthed from a tomb in Xian. They are identical and have clearly been cast from a mould, a strangely appropriate finding given China's current manufacturing reputation. Chinese society flowers later, however, and along different lines from Western society.

These four civilisations – the Mesopotamian, Egyptian, Indian, and Chinese – are the great societies of prehistory, and much of what we understand, especially about their need for display, has to be educated guesswork. But it seems that depic-

tions of human genitalia, the penis in particular, were important to our ancestors, on all sorts of levels. The modern genital
exhibitionist, male or female, may be following an instinct that
goes back to the dawn of time. As does the instinct to display
one's wealth and power in building or the acquisition of gold
and jewels.

The civilisation that succeeded them, Ancient Greece, flourished in the seven centuries before the birth of Christ, leaving a
legacy which has survived into the modern world. From the
eighth century BC until it came under the rule of Rome in
146BC, the Hellenic civilisation established the disciplines of
architecture, art, drama, philosophy, mathematics, science,
sculpture and politics, among many others. It gained an
empire, with Alexander, and sowed the seed of its intellectual
brilliance throughout the Mediterranean and Near East, with
ideas that are still relevant today. The thoughts of Aristotle,
Plato and Socrates, Euclid and Pythagoras remain the bedrock
for philosophy and science, virtually every major city in the
world has buildings constructed in the Classical style, and few
sculptors have equalled the mastery of the Ancient Greeks, let
alone surpassed it. The Ancient Greeks laid the template for the
life of the mind.

The origins of their society are obscure, probably arising
from contact with Egypt and the Near East, but from the outset
they were different. Like other civilisations, they had their
pantheon of gods, but the Greek gods were not remote or
strange to behold, but recognisably human, both in their
personalities and their actions. Zeus, the father of the gods,
behaves more like a dirty old man than an omnipotent deity,
forever trying to seduce other Goddesses and human women,
as well as boys. The tales of the gods are full of rape, murder,
cannibalism and pederasty, and there is hardly an event that
does not begin with some sexual misadventure. The complex
web of relationships this reveals is very human in its construction, particularly in the unintended consequences of impulsive
behaviour. The Greek myths bring the gods down to Earth.

The Greek pantheon was therefore well versed in the arts of love, and two gods in particular symbolise uncomplicated male virility. Pan lives in the wilderness and is the god of shepherds, huntsman and rustic music. His association with nature and the seasons linked him with fertility, and he had the reputation as a great lover. He played a characteristic set of pipes, which are still used by folk and street musicians today. He is often portrayed with an erect penis, and in later depictions has a goat's horns and legs.

The minor god Priapus, possibly the son of Pan, was thrown off Olympus for being ugly and is *always* depicted with a huge, permanently erect, penis. He, too, was associated with fertility and was seen as a protector of land and a bringer of good luck. For that reason he is sometimes associated with fishermen and sailors. Statues of Priapus were erected to protect land and were often hung with slogans and slang poetry to warn off trespassers. In these, Priapus would threaten to rape any woman and sodomise any man who sought to commit a crime within the boundaries. The sexual language is coarse and explicit, and the tone would not be out of place in some of the rougher parts of our society. Well into the Christian era, statues of Priapus were used to promote health and fertility, one of the few Greek gods who has survived as a working deity. The only other one regularly invoked is Apollo, the God of healing, who appears at the start of the Hippocratic Oath, the doctor's code: 'I swear by Apollo, the God of healing … '. Even Apollo, though, does not have the popularity of Priapus, models of whom appear in every gift shop throughout Greece.

The importance of Ancient Greece to the story of exhibitionism does not depend solely on its depictions of the gods, but in the history of its society. For the first time we get names of people who are not just mythical or legendary but recognisable human beings. Aristotle, Plato, Alexander, Demosthenes and Socrates were all distinct individuals whose thoughts and actions can be examined through contemporary historical record. Homer was the world's first author, although 'his' stories, the Iliad and the Odyssey, were probably collaborative works.

It was in Ancient Greece that we first had reliable evidence of people performing for entertainment, and also for power and reward. The earliest record of athletic games dates back to about 760BC, although whether they were the origins of the Olympics remains in doubt. What we do know is that at a later date the athletes competed naked, in order that judges could better assess their style and physicality. (They trained at the gymnasium, 'gymnos' being Greek for naked.) The Olympiads also featured competitions for poetry, sculpture and dance, all of which carried the promise of reward. The exhibition of artistic and sporting prowess became a means of self-enrichment.

Although many of the names have been lost, we also know the identities of some of the most famous Ancient Greek artists. Phidias the sculptor designed the Parthenon, and Praxiteles became famous for his sculptures of the female nude. We have the names of about one hundred poets and playwrights, the most famous being Aristophanes, Aeschylus, Euripides and Sophocles. The first actor was Thespis and, later we have the names of Choerilus and Phrynichus. The first plays were tragedies, and owed their origin to old fertility cults – tragos is Greek for goat, and ode means song. So both meanings for exhibitionism – genital display and 'exhibiting' or public performance – go back to the same root.

Comedies were a later invention, and involved political satire and sexual innuendo, mocking the exalted and hoi polloi alike. Aristophanes is the best known of the authors, creating a model that has survived into modern times. One of his works, *Clouds,* has a satirical portrait of the philosopher Socrates, demonstrating comedy's unique power to irritate and humble the great and good. Making people laugh is often inseparable from intended or unintended exhibitionism, and the stand-up comedian has a place all of his or her own in the performing arts.

The importance of public performance to Greek society can be measured by the profusion of theatres, whose ruins can be found dotted throughout the Mediterranean. Another branch of performance that has survived to the present day is the art of rhetoric. In its pure form, it means the ability to develop arguments verbally and was widely taught to enable students to master skills in philosophy, politics and law. Aristotle was one of the many philosophers who recorded the basic skills of rhetoric, which he divided into three component parts – ethos, or how the character and experience of the speaker can give them gravitas; pathos, the use of metaphor and storytelling to make emotional appeals to the audience; and logos, the use of reasoning to make an argument. Rhetoric was held to be one of the most important ways, if not the most important, of preserving the Athenian democracy. It follows that the ability to perform in public, to exhibit one's self, and to maintain composure were key skills for the Athenian men of power. Demosthenes, the most famous of the Greek orators, was said to practice his skills assiduously, cultivating his voice and using his body expressively. His critics accused him of excessive theatricality, in other words, of being an exhibitionist. Although we now have many people who declaim to the public through the media in its various guises, the art of rhetoric, the ability to construct a logic argument and establish dialectic in an entertaining and coherent fashion has almost disappeared from public life, to the impoverishment of our society. It is perhaps still practised in Parliament, but probably only when the chamber is nearly empty, and certainly not during Prime Minister's Questions.

Exhibitionism could also be the result of spending an afternoon at the Symposium, the male drinking clubs where poetry was recited and homosexuality practiced. The spirit of Dionysius, the Greek god of wine, was never far from Greek theatre, and symposia often degenerated into a drunken rampage through the town. And note that they were men – art, politics and the theatre were all the preserve of Athenian men, with women and slaves considered second-class citizens. The origins of the artistic exhibitionist, therefore, are found in the civilisation of Ancient Greece, who left us a legacy of artistic and sporting performance, as well as intellectual brilliance.

When we get to Rome, however, the word that springs to mind is 'power', for if Rome could not better Greece in its art and philosophy, it certainly could in terms of its empire, its engineering and its law. If the Greeks exhibited their intellect then the Romans exhibited their might, and left behind concrete evidence of their power and majesty.

It was Augustus, the first Roman Emperor, who began the construction boom that would transform Rome. He ruled from 27BC to AD14, and in that time he, 'inherited a city of mud brick and left it a city of marble.' Although the creation of an Emperor ran against the founding principles of the republic, the office had one great benefit for posterity – only the Emperor had the ability and the means to initiate large-scale building projects. Augustus seems to have been a contradiction – on the one hand he was the most powerful ruler the world had ever seen, yet he preferred to live frugally without ostentation. And like many great and clever men, he did not grab power, but created the circumstances whereby Rome needed an Emperor, with himself as the obvious choice. The Senate offered him the position, he did not create it, although by that time his power was so great that to refuse him would have been unwise. Aside from his ability, he had the support of the army – a vital tool in the establishment of a dictatorship – a powerful network of friends and plenty of money. He was therefore almost unassailable, which in itself is a form of exhibitionism if you think about it. (Socrates predicted this inevitable descent of democracy into tyranny in Plato's work *The Republic*, where he argued that the freedoms gained under democracy would lead to social unrest, and the call for a strong leader to restore order. A modern allegory of the process can be seen in the *Star Wars* series of films.)

Augustus inaugurated a building programme that made Rome beautiful. Roman engineers used Luna marble to clothe buildings and it is said that over 80 temples were refurbished in Augustus' time. He established a police force and fire fighters for Rome, and was generous in his support of the poor and military veterans. Through his victorious military leadership he extended the Empire and, more importantly, gave Roman citizens an extended period of peace.

From the time of Augustus, the Roman emperors used construction to exhibit their power and importance. Nero had a statue of himself built which was over 120 feet high. This was later refashioned in their own image by succeeding emperors, including Commodus, the weak emperor made famous by Ridley Scott's film *Gladiator*. And sport, gladiatorial contests and entertainments were the Emperor's main gift to their people.

Gladiatorial contests took place in the Coliseum, the famous stadium in the heart of Rome, built in the first century AD by the Emperor Vespasian. To maintain their position, the Roman emperors had to juggle the various factions seeking to usurp them, as well as keeping the populace happy. The ordinary citizen was apparently simple and fickle – *'Duas tantum res anxius optat, Panem et Circences'* ('Only two things does he anxiously wish for, bread and circuses'), wrote the poet Juvenal. The Coliseum, home to wild animals, gladiators and even sea battles, was an exhibition of the emperor's regard for his people. Nobody in real life ever said that 'Rome is the mob', but it was true, that, 'he who controls the mob, controls Rome'. A popular emperor was a safe emperor. At its height the Coliseum could house 50,000 people, making it bigger than many modern stadia. The nearby Circus Maximus, scene of chariot races and other entertainments, could accommodate – it is estimated – nearly 150,000 people. Nothing succeeds like excess.

The exhibition of Roman power was also found in the awarding of a 'triumph' to a victorious general. This usually followed a successful foreign war, although was later modified to include single battles of sufficient size. The triumph took the form of a procession through Rome, led by the Senate, with the spoils of war and captives displayed on carts, the victorious general and his legions feted by the crowds. The significant triumphs took place before the creation of the empire, when the Senate decided who should qualify. After the establishment of an empire, only the Emperor could be awarded a full triumph, and the practice slowly died out. It is important because this kind of public display was, until relatively recently, a staple of Communist countries (and still is in North Korea). The annual May Day celebration in the old USSR was primarily an exhibition of the armed might of the Soviet Union, but also a display of political importance, as figures who had fallen out of favour disappeared from the Kremlin balcony. And from history – their faces were airbrushed out of old photographs to make it appear as if they had never existed.

Roman society was similar to Greek, being dominated by men, although the class divisions were more complex. At the bottom of society were the slaves, just up from them were the freedmen, and above them the citizens, who were either patricians – descended from one of the hundred founding families – or plebeians. Women were still second-class citizens, rarely venturing beyond their home, although among the patrician class there was some social intermingling.

As far as sex was concerned Roman society was similar to the Greek, and although we have a view of them as famously debauched this was true only for certain periods, notably in the century following Augustus. One would expect some form of sexual exhibitionism to have been rife in Rome but, apart from some explicit mosaics, there is little to differentiate them from other ancient societies. There does seem to have been a thriving phallic cult – hundreds of phallic objects were found at Pompeii – but generally the mores of the society were similar to Greek civilisation.

We remember Rome for its empire and the ruins of imperial power that it left for posterity. Perhaps its greatest legacy, certainly as far as the modern world is concerned, was the embrace of Christianity by the empire in the fourth century AD. Over the centuries, Christianity developed as a strongly moral religion, absorbing the lessons of the Old Testament, including the Ten Commandments, and adding a few of its own through the teaching of St Paul. The society which lived by this code would be monotheistic, monogamous, sexually chaste and free from crime and idolatry. One could exhibit one's piety, but very little else, and for the first time the poor and humble were seen to be leading a better life than the rich and famous.

One of the more interesting facets of Christianity is the contrast between the teachings of Jesus, which have very little to say on the matter of sex, and the numerous interpretations of his teachings which have followed since. Christians were encouraged to lead pure, simple and humble lives. Many early Christians interpreted this as a call to shun society and they led anonymous lives as hermits in the desert, a sort of anti-exhibitionism. Although even this was open to the temptations of celebrity. What are we to make, for example, of Simon Stylites, who lived on top of a pole in the desert for thirty years and became famous for his piety? Isn't that exhibitionism – 'Look at me, look how holy I am'? These are deep waters.

The other great monotheistic religion to arise in the first millennium AD was Islam, which – like Christianity – gives guidance to its followers as to how to live according to sacred teachings. Islam goes further than Christianity in specifying a dress code for women, although it is important to realise that this is interpreted differently in different countries, and in different branches of the faith. Judaism, the oldest monotheistic religion of them all, also gives general advice as to how to conduct oneself, both in terms of social interaction and self-respect. By the end of the first millennium of the Christian era, all three religions would be providing a moral framework for the majority of the world's population.

In India, Hinduism was growing, and although it is an aggregate of beliefs and deities rather than a single monotheistic entity, one of its ubiquitous beliefs is the law of karma, which could be roughly translated as, 'what goes around, comes around'. In other words, it is in your interest to behave properly, because your actions will return to haunt you. Buddhism takes this further, stating that if one ignores the law of karma, you are destined to be trapped on the wheel of samsara, or earthly reincarnation, forever. Those who wish to gain enlightenment must live correctly, for the impure in mind, speech or action can never attain nirvana. All these religions, which together now influence the majority of the world's population, have the notion of 'good' or 'right' behaviour versus 'bad' or 'unskilful' behaviour. And bad behaviour for all of them usually encompasses adultery, murder, stealing, lust and depravity, along with worshipping graven images and all sorts of other indiscretions including sexual exhibitionism.

The Christian attitude to nudity is influenced – I don't think that you can put it any stronger than this – by the story of Adam and Eve. You will recall that God created Adam from dust and 'breathed life into him', and later created Eve from Adam's rib. They lived, naked, in the Garden of Eden and could eat 'from any tree' save one, the tree of knowledge, because, 'the day thou eatest thereof thou shalt surely die'. But the serpent, 'the most subtle of God's creatures,' persuades Eve to eat the fruit of the tree of knowledge. She shares the fruit with Adam and the 'eyes of both of them were opened, and they knew that they *were* naked; and they sewed fig leaves together and made themselves aprons.' I have quoted the story at length because this page of the Bible has had more psychological impact on Christian (and Jewish) society than virtually anything else. God gives mankind a paradise to live in with one proviso, that they don't do one specific thing. The woman – this is very significant – is beguiled by the serpent (!) and eats the forbidden fruit, persuading Adam to eat it as well. Afterwards they see the material world as it really is, find their nakedness embarrassing, and for that they have to leave the Garden of Eden. Paradise is lost due to Eve's lapse, and mankind's turbulent earthly history begins.

For our Western and nominally Christian society, the story of sexual exhibitionism can be seen to begin here. If nakedness is normal, there is nothing to exhibit and the whole thing becomes meaningless. Also, look at the other psychological factors which present here. 'You can eat from any tree save one, the tree of knowledge'. If that isn't a loaded invitation to transgress, then what is? But even then you won't do it because you *know* it's wrong, until that little voice in your head (the serpent) says, 'go on, do it'. And you do it, and instantly you regret it, and feel shame and remorse, but it is no good because *you can't go back.* That is what is so powerful about the story of Adam and Eve; the notion of paradise lost. And how many times in our own lives have we been through this scenario, when we break a diet, cadge a cigarette, or otherwise do something which we know is wrong? We may have shaken off religion but the old templates for temptation and guilt are still there, driving the impulse to behave badly.

The period from the fall of the Roman Empire to the beginning of the medieval era is generally known as the Dark Ages in Britain, because we understand so little about it. It is difficult to picture a society which has left few buildings and hardly any written records. However, the period may have been the source of two remarkable representations in the history of genital exhibitionism.

The first is the Cerne Abbas giant, a male figure with an erect phallus carved into a hill in Dorset. It may not date from this time, however, and is probably an unreliable indication of Dark Age belief. The second, though, is far more interesting – the Sheelagh Na Gig figures found carved on churches throughout Europe, but mainly in Britain and Ireland. Sheelagh is a carved stone female figure with a grossly enlarged vagina, the labia of which she is often pulling apart. The effect is vulgar bordering on the grotesque, and almost horrifying. The most famous

Sheelagh in Britain is found on the wall of a church in Kilpeck, near Hereford, which has a variety of other curved heads and figurines known as the Corbals. She is thought to be an old Celtic fertility symbol, which seems to be polite society's best way of explaining these violently lewd images. Depictions of naked men, again in a state of arousal, are also found on churches throughout Europe, and again probably have their origin in Pagan times.

As we move into the medieval period we see again the use of building to exhibit power. The best example occurs here in Britain, where the Norman conquerors marked their authority in stone. Nothing remains now of the old Saxon wooden halls, but the great castles and abbeys of Norman England are still here, massive and enduring. Over 500 castles were built by the Normans, including the Tower of London, and they were still being built 200 years later. The reason behind them was simple. At the time of the invasion, it was estimated that there were only 10,000 Normans trying to hold down a native population of nearly two million. The castles were secure bases for troops to control the scattered settlements of England but, more importantly, they were a statement – 'Look at what we can do, look at our power'. The Normans were not a rumour or a fleeting presence but right there in front of you, a ruthless invader prepared to exhibit his might. And the great Norman abbeys of England with their huge naves, massive columns and soaring heights were another exhibition, a rich, powerful society demonstrating to the heathens what worship was really about.

The abbeys and churches were the centres of learning, and probably the main repository of any cultural history of the period. Unfortunately most of it has been lost due to the passage of time and the Reformation, when the cultural history of England was destroyed. Enough remains, however, to leave us with a picture of early medieval society, which indicates a bucolic, rural society, probably more civilised than we appreciate, but certainly bawdy. The great monastic foundations came about in order to isolate the pious from the depravity of ordinary life. A Benedictine monk, Thomas Brinton, thought the Black Plague which devastated fourteenth-century England was God's answer to the debauched society of those times. This century also saw England's first work of literature, Chaucer's *Canterbury Tales*, which contains at least one episode of 'mooning' among its vivid and bawdy representations of medieval England. And further afield, in Venice in the 1550s, a man called Domenego was sentenced to six months in prison for, 'repeated display of his pudendal member'. This is the first recorded instance of a man receiving legal punishment for exposing himself.

While the histories have very little to say on the matter of sexual exhibitionism in the early Middle Ages, the matter of public display undergoes a revolution. Gothic architecture transforms the ecclesiastical buildings of Europe, adding elegance to the solid power of the Norman abbeys. Stained glass transforms the interiors of these gloomy abbeys, as the great east and west windows of our cathedrals testify. The eye is drawn to the light and to the ceiling, to heaven.

In Italy in the fifteenth century, something even more impressive was happening. The Renaissance was taking place in painting and sculpture, a rebirth of the themes of classical antiquity. The great names of this time – Michelangelo and Leonardo – and thousands of others would, in less than 200 years, transform sculpture and painting, and recreate the Ancient Greek veneration for the decorative arts. A transformation occurs from the flat, anonymous, religious works of the Middle Ages to the vivid canvases and sculptures of the Renaissance. Most importantly, we get a body of work and styles which are linked with a single individual. The whole Machiavellian world of commercial art is born.

While Domenego was exposing himself in Venice, something quite different was happening in England: the social, religious and economic revolution known as the Reformation. It began with Pope Clement VII refusing to annul Henry VIII's first marriage, which led to Henry throwing off the authority of the Pope and creating the Church of England. In the process he dissolved the monasteries, appropriating their wealth to the Crown, and laid the ground for England's adoption of the simpler Protestant faith which was sweeping through Europe. This is a hugely important event in the history of exhibitionism in its broadest sense. The 'protest' in Protestantism was against the corruption of the established Catholic Church, which by the sixteenth century was ostentatiously wealthy, both in land and possessions.

Churches and abbeys were richly decorated with paintings, fine tapestries, and statuary. The clergy were clothed in silk and jewels, and some were famously debauched, hardly bothering to make a pretence of sobriety or celibacy. Cardinal Wolsley, Henry VIII's Lord Chancellor, commissioned a report into the state of the monasteries, which detailed numerous impieties, among them drunkenness, lechery, gambling and gluttony. And worse still, for the true believers, were the bizarre manipulations of faith practiced by the hierarchy. One of them was the sale of indulgences, whereby you paid the clergy to reduce your time in Purgatory after you died. It was Martin Luther's critique of this practice, nailed to a church in Wittenberg, which sparked the Reformation.

The effect, in England, was startling. Churches and monasteries were stripped of their plate, jewels and finery. The monasteries lost their land and the monks were driven out, leaving the buildings to rot. Many churches had wall paintings or frescos which were whitewashed over or left as bare stone. Paintings and statues were looted or destroyed. Although the monetary gain to Henry VIII was considerable, the primary motive was religious, a move to clear away the saints, relics and icons and restore a clear view to heaven. Religious exhibitionism was destroyed in an iconoclastic orgy which the historian Andrew Graham-Dixon called: 'the greatest act of vandalism in the history of art'.

It was in this era that the ground rules of morality in society were formed. The old Catholic Church had, in many respects, been fairly tolerant; well suited to bucolic England with its 'live and let live' approach. The arrival of Protestantism, with its more puritanical view both of religion and morality, caused a fundamental change in British society. A cyclical pattern emerged, veering between overtly moral eras like the Commonwealth, the Victorians and post-war Britain, and more licentious times, like the Regency period, the 1920s or the 1960s.

Politically, the next 400 years were to see Britain transformed, becoming a global maritime power through sailors like Drake and Raleigh. This in turn led to the emergence of a mercantile class who became very wealthy, and are important because they acquired status outside of the traditional pathways to prosperity and preferment. And they displayed their wealth in great houses and sponsorship of the arts – it was not enough to be rich, one must be seen to be rich. One must be 'one of us'.

The Elizabethan era gave us Shakespeare, whose revolutionary plays explored the complexities of the human psyche as well as the social mores of time, giving us a considerably more sophisticated version of relationships than bawdy Chaucer. It began the great theatrical tradition of England, which encompassed fame for individual actors and writers, and prefaced the huge influence that the performing arts have upon our lives.

Elizabethan England also saw the emergence of a more complex legal system, notably the need to provide protection for the poor. The poor were classified into three categories: the impotent, who could not work and needed care; the able bodied, who were sent to a House of Industry; and the idle poor, who were sent to a House of Correction, or prison. A later attempt to deal with the problem of the idle poor, the 1824 Vagrancy Act, would make it an offence for a man to, 'wilfully, openly, lewdly and obscenely expose his person, in any street, road or public highway, or in the view thereof, or in any place of public resort, with intent to insult any female. It shall be lawful for the Justice of the Peace to commit him to a House of Correction for any time not exceeding than three calendar months.'

The need to make specific reference to male genital exposure indicated that the problem was well known, although the offence could only previously be dealt with under the charge of 'disturbing the King's peace'. One of the most famous prosecutions under this law took place in 1663 and concerned Sir Charles Sedley: courtier, wit, and later speaker of the House of Commons. He and his friends got drunk at the Cock (!) Tavern in Bow Street and went out to the balcony, where Sir Charles took his clothes off and indulged in 'blasphemous and obscene antics', which so offended the gathering crowd that they were arrested. Sir Charles, who was well connected, only suffered a week's imprisonment.

Sir Charles was living in a time of great intellectual change, known as the Enlightenment, when scientific methods and discoveries were challenging superstition and religious certainties about the nature of the world. Before the nineteenth century, sexual exhibitionism was considered only as a sin, with little or no thought given to the psychological state of the sinner. From the late eighteenth century, however, enlightened physicians on the continent and in the Americas started looking more closely at people whose actions and personalities fell outside the boundaries of accepted behaviour, usually labelled as 'lunatics' or 'idiots'. The discipline of psychiatry was born and had its first flowering in Germany, where disease classifications and treatments were pioneered. This was part of a wider medical enlightenment, when science emerged to challenge the religious superstitions and certainties of the time.

The Victorian age also saw great social changes as the rural population flocked to the industrial cities. London had one million people in 1800; by 1912 this was seven million. Industrialisation also saw the disappearance of individual trades like shoemaking, now done by machines. Moving to a city and working a machine was a far cry from 'merrie England' and seemed to effect a profound psychological shift in the population. There were hardly any asylums in 1800; by 1900 there were hundreds, and they were all full.

It was a Parisian physician, Charles Lasègue, who in 1877 first described sexual exhibitionism as a distinct clinical entity. He recorded that these exhibitionists were men of previously good character, who, while not suffering from overt signs of mental illness, could not be described as mentally healthy. This is important because offenders could now be regarded as patients in need of treatment, rather than just sinners. And although the origins of psychology lie back in the seventeenth century, it is really from this point on that the modern science gathers momentum. Lasègue wrote that many psychological disorders sprang from the 'ictus', the moment in the person's life when the balance of his mind was disturbed. From then on, his mind is like, 'a piano with certain keys removed, which when played will result in only dissonant and imperfect chords.'

The world's first psychological laboratory was created in Germany in 1879, and psychology as a discipline swept through Europe and the USA. Sigmund Freud started his career in 1885, and focussed his attention on the history of the patient, looking for events and relationships as the keys to the patient's mental state, a discipline which became known as psychoanalysis. His disciple Jung went further, refining, and rejecting some of Freud's work, and laying the template for our modern understanding of personality types. Although human beings have probably always regarded each other as essentially individuals, society had long believed in simpler categories: saint or sinner; healthy or unhealthy; mad or sane. The scientific Enlightenment and the revolution in behavioural science, which mushroomed in the late-twentieth century, demonstrated an altogether more complex picture. The sexual exhibitionist was still a sinner, but also mentally ill.

Public display was, by the mid-twentieth century, firmly established in the social firmament. There are theatres, art galleries, sports grounds and concert halls, and a thriving literary scene. And yet there is a huge gap between 'high art' and the more egalitarian branches of each discipline. Outside of local dramatic societies, acting belonged in the theatre, or on the radio, and – apart from comedians – probably did not affect that many people. Similarly art became the preserve of the upper middle classes and, again, barely troubled the vast majority of the population. The great stately homes of England, the very essence of gracious living, became a favoured Sunday afternoon day out, but why they were built, and what it says about those who built them probably didn't matter to the vast majority of visitors. British society, and maybe Western society as a whole, was structured, narrow minded, law abiding, religious and suspicious of most forms of 'showing off', as exhibitionism was called. And then along came the 1960s and everything changed, the nature of which will be dealt with in the following chapters. But first, we need to consider more closely the person who springs to mind when exhibitionism is mentioned, the rogue male in his dirty raincoat who haunts our parks and alleyways, and whether he is really just a pervert, whether he is mentally ill, or indeed whether he is doing something that harks back to the dawn of time.

3

Sexual exhibitionism

In the past chapter we have seen sexual exhibitionism as an evolving story, starting as part of human ritual and display, then becoming a criminal offence, and finally being defined as an illness. As mankind becomes more civilised, it seems we also become more prudish, or at least, more prone to embarrassment. The psychological baggage of Adam and Eve still haunts us.

We do not know what prompted ancient man to carve phallic symbols, or early medieval craftsmen to fashion Sheelagh na Gig figures on Europe's churches. What we do know is that from the seventeenth century onwards, exposing one's genitalia became defined as an act of public lewdness, and was dealt with initially as a disturbance of the peace and then as a separate law. The first law in England to specifically name genital exposure was the 1824 Vagrancy Act, and there have been amendments ever since, notably the 1956 and 2003 Sexual Offences Acts. Most other civilised countries have similar laws relating to genital exhibitionism, although tolerance varies widely, even between individual states in the USA. Despite the fact that getting one's kit off in public has become more acceptable, especially if you are female and the audience is composed of slavering men, 'flashing' is still generally taboo. Western society lurches from puritanism to licentiousness, but some things remain beyond the pale.

One of the interesting things about modern society is the way these old problems keep recurring, as if we cannot eradicate some basic human instinct. Public morality is cyclical, but problems like exhibitionism never seem to go away. Perhaps it is connected to one of the dominant traits of European civilisation, our nostalgia for a forgotten life. For as long as I can remember, people have harked back to some mythical age, usually the one immediately predating their childhood, a place where the machine age has been edited out. The recent financial disasters have reinforced the belief among some of us that we have lost touch with both our inner selves and the ancient rhythms of nature, and that we should return to an older, simpler existence.

There could be a grain of truth in this recurring folk memory. If one looks beneath the great sweep of history, with its kings and queens and wars and treaties, you could make a good case for the quality of life before the Industrial Revolution. Monty Python member Terry Jones, in his book and TV series *Medieval Lives*, thought that the traditional description of a medieval peasant's life as 'nasty, brutish and short' was quite wrong. He thought that they had a balanced existence, with plenty of 'holy days', saint's days and feasts to provide entertainment. And they would have been fun, as the medieval Briton – like his modern counterpart – probably only needed alcohol and a bit of music to have a good time. Feudal law was brutal, but the lords in their castles would not have been bothered overmuch by the antics of the peasantry. Which was just as well because, to adapt the saying of H. L. Menken, nobody ever lost money by underestimating the taste of the British public. The echo of the simple pastoral life, where we were freer and less constrained to behave 'properly' has a powerful resonance in our busy lives.

The advent of the Industrial Revolution saw all that change as the population moved to the towns and cities for work, and the laws that govern human behaviour began to take shape. Having a pee in a hedge is one thing, but openly urinating or defecating in a busy street is quite another. And slowly the building blocks of modern Britain grew, street by street, law by law. As the poet Richard Lovelace had it:

> *Stone walls do not a prison make,*
> *Nor iron bars a cage*

As we explored in the last chapter, the age of the machine ushered in the birth of psychology and I think it is fair to assume that as society became more complex, so human beings became more prone to psychological distress. One of the biggest growth industries in the post-war years has been the mushrooming of personal and spiritual self-help books, offering answers to the dislocation of modern life. Religions, both mainstream and alternative, offer solutions to the stresses of existence, using ancient techniques such as prayer and meditation to calm the insistent, ambient noise of civilisation. And there is this great pressure to conform, paradoxically much greater in the information age than it was even when I was young. We were not relentlessly tested as schoolchildren are now, having education rammed into them in often joyless schools where teachers operate in a climate of fear. In my profession, medicine, you could try a couple of specialities before making a choice, something which would be career suicide now. (You also treated patients as individuals, not collections of statistics who had to be fed pills till the numbers were right.) The modern world is on at everybody, especially the young, telling them what will happen if they don't conform. Even rebellion has been tidied up into Facebook and the mobile phone.

Enter the exhibitionist. What exactly is he doing, this young recidivist? Because he will be young, and the likelihood is that he will reoffend until he gets caught. Is he some sort of folk hero, defying convention and going down in a blaze of publicity? Or is he a throwback, a person with part of his primitive hindbrain still functioning, following some forgotten ancient ritual? Or is he just a pervert, one of those people whose sexual instincts have been warped and turned into something unhealthy?

One thing is for certain; exhibitionism is, statistically, the most common sexual offence. The psychoanalyst Brett Kahr, in his study of exhibitionism, reckoned indecent exposure accounted for about a third of reported sexual offences, which in 2011 in England would have numbered 6,500 instances alone. The key word when dealing with any form of sexual offence is 'reported', as the vast majority of incidents never become known. Studies using groups of women such as students or nurses show between 30 and 50 per cent of women had been the victims of a 'flasher', and up to 60 per cent knew of someone who had been a victim. The majority of these victims, over three quarters, did not report the crime. That is not to say the victims were unharmed by the experience. The studies which have been done show that although it can be regarded as relatively mild experience for some women, for others it can be a shocking event which leaves lasting mental scars. In the popular imagination male genital exhibitionism has an element of bathos to it, as if it is somehow just pathetic or amusing. Maybe so, but it has its dark side.

Nowhere is this more evident than in the personality of the exposer. Charles Lasègue, the first person to describe the condition, defined exhibitionism as: 'a sudden urge to display one's genitalia in a public forum'. He noted that they were men, previously of good character, who showed no desire to pursue a further relationship with the women, and who had little or no insight into the condition. He defined their mental state as: 'somewhere between reason and madness', which, by the standards of the time was an accurate description. They could neither be described as entirely sane, nor completely mad, their actions being bizarre but not associated with symptoms of psychosis such as hallucinations or delusions.

The definition of an exhibitionist in the American Psychiatric Association's *Diagnostic and Statistical Manual of Mental*

Disorders, fourth edition (DSM IV), comes under the heading of 'Sexual and Gender Identity Disorders'. There are three categories to this classification: the *sexual dysfunctions*, where there is malfunctioning of the genital organs; the *paraphilias*, where there is an aberration of the sex act or the sex object; and the *gender identity disorders*, like transvestism or transsexuality.

Exhibitionism is a paraphilia and is a deviation of the sex act; in other words, sexual satisfaction is gained from genital exposure rather than consensual intercourse. Voyeurism is similar. Paraphilic deviations of the sexual object include fetishism and paedophilia. The DSM IV defines an exhibitionist as someone who, 'experiences recurrent, intense, and sexually arousing behaviours or fantasies of genital exposure to an unsuspecting stranger. The behaviours or fantasies must have endured for at least six months to receive a psychiatric diagnosis. Furthermore, the behaviours or fantasies or urges must cause clinically significant distress or impairment to the individual's social or occupational functioning, or to other areas of life.' In other words these men are not performing a one-off act as a bit of harmless fun, but are compelled to repeat something that, if witnessed, would utterly ruin their lives. It is Eve and the apple all over again.

Male genital exhibitionists fall into two categories. Type 1 exposes himself by unzipping his fly to reveal his penis, which is normally flaccid. The act is usually done quickly and the perpetrator is silent, exposing himself then disappearing. The second, type 2, is more aggressive, displaying an erect penis and often openly masturbating. He may talk to his victims, making obscene remarks or suggestions. Type 1 often feels intense shame or remorse, whereas type 2 doesn't, some apparently even feeling a certain sense of pride. It comes as no surprise to learn that type 2 exhibitionists are more dangerous to their victims and more likely to commit other crimes.

So who are these exhibitionists, and where do they come from? There are a significant number of case reports and from these a few conclusions can be drawn. A relaxed family attitude to nudity is found in some cases, with one patient describing how his mother would come into the bathroom, naked, to fix her hair while he was in the bath. And she would come in and urinate, as would his father, again while he was in the room. A girl who got into trouble for taking her clothes off at a party described how her mother would walk round the house naked. There are not a great many of these cases, but there are enough to make them interesting.

Much more common in the history of genital exhibitionism is a history of abuse or family dysfunction. The comprehensive work on the subject, *Sexual Deviance: Theory, Assessment and Treatment*, edited by Richard Laws and William O'Donahue, shows exhibitionists are more likely than the general population to have a history of childhood mental illness, physical or mental abuse and juvenile criminality. Even if they do not have overt childhood problems, they are still more likely to have come from dysfunctional families, which could include sibling bullying, marital breakup and parental death. As many other conditions also spring from the above circumstances, one cannot be definitive about their predictability for exhibitionism. Charles Lasègue spoke of men 'of good character', but modern research has indicated that they are more likely to come from disturbed backgrounds. Moreover, their flashing career usually begins early, and although they may be pillars of the community when caught, most will have a long history of unreported exhibitionism.

Most exhibitionists – about two thirds – are married, and they are drawn from all social groups. They also suffer from other paraphilias; about a third enjoy voyeurism and another third practice frottage, that is rubbing themselves against someone in a crowd to gain sexual satisfaction. More seriously, about 15 per cent of exhibitionists have been convicted for rape. Genital exposure does not bring much joy either – nearly 90 per cent of sufferers having a mood disorder like anxiety or depression.

The American psychiatrist Martin Kafka, an expert on the paraphilias, believes many exhibitionists and voyeurs also suffer from a variety of other problems, such as compulsive masturbation, promiscuity, pornography dependence, cybersex (internet) addiction and telephone sex. He found a link with Attention Deficit Hyperactivity Disorder (ADHD), which presented as hypersexuality in people with the paraphilias. There was also a link between paraphilia and crime, both sexual and non-sexual. Many also had drug and alcohol problems.

The picture we have so far is of a young man, married, who may have a family history of tolerating nudity. That family is likely, however, to have had problems, and the young man may well have been the victim of either physical or emotional abuse. He is very likely to be clinically depressed and is more likely to have substance abuse issues. He will have started his exhibitionist career in his teens and will almost certainly have been a multiple offender before he is caught. He may be relatively harmless, but is more likely to have other issues around sexuality and may even be a frank criminal. He may suffer shame and remorse, but equally may exhibit no shame at all, almost depersonalising his victims. In general, it can be said that the act of self-exposure is a declaration of a disturbed personality.

Formal psychology recognises various personality disorders, and it is surprisingly difficult to place the exhibitionist within a convenient pigeonhole. The neurotic personality, for whom anxiety is a constant companion, can develop obsessive compulsions, although these do not tend to include bizarre acts like exhibitionism. Schizoid personalities, who live in a fantasy world, might fit but they are often deeply disturbed, while the exhibitionist tends to be otherwise unremarkable. The psychopath's complete disregard for others is a feature of type 2 exhibitionism but, again, their psychopathic tendencies are across the board, not a picture consistent with the majority of exhibitionists.

So what causes it? The answer is that nobody knows, although there are numerous theories. For a long time it would have been considered as simply a sin, a manifestation of evil, an illustration of the power of Satan to corrupt human minds. As we shall see when relating a case story, there could be something in this, as some exhibitionists feel that they are not in full control of their actions. And in our more tolerant society, one must also ask the question, is it really an abnormality, a crime, or merely a variant of common behaviour? The next edition of the *Diagnostic and Statistical Manual of Mental Disorders* (DSM V), due out in 2013, may answer the question, reclassifying some aspects of the paraphilias. For the moment, though, it is sufficient to stick to the current definition, that it is a sexual disorder.

Charles Lasègue identified the disorder in 1877 and other early psychiatrists and psychotherapists began to consider the problems caused by mental dysfunction. The man who laid the groundwork for the workings of the mind was Sigmund Freud and although much of his work has been questioned and revised, no one can deny the scope and detail of his theories. Freud attached great importance to the fact that we were born naked and observed that it was quite normal for three and four year old children to exhibit their body parts. Freud himself remembers urinating in front of his parents when he was eight and his father remarking that, 'the boy will come to nothing'. It seems that some form of exhibitionism is normal for male children. As we mature this exhibitionism is repressed as part of the transition to normal adulthood.

Freud saw exhibitionism as a 'vicissitude' or a twisting, of the sex instincts. He wrote a complex essay on 'Instincts and their Vicissitudes', which is difficult to summarise in a short book, but the general theory is that there are numerous sexual instincts and their aim is ultimately 'organ pleasure'. They are also, 'distinguished by possessing the capacity to act vicariously for one another … .and to change their object readily'. This means that instincts are capable of functions which are far removed from their original purpose, and can therefore undergo the following vicissitudes:

- Reversal into its opposite
- Turning round upon the subject's own self
- Repression
- Sublimation

Exhibitionism is, in Freud's view, an example of the first process, where an active principle – to look at – is replaced by its passive opposite – to be looked at. And the exhibitionist is a 'pervert', someone who acts on their instincts as opposed to the neurotic, who merely fantasises and never acts. (The trouble with Freud is that, once you start, you plunge into this forest of theories and concepts, and it is very easy to get lost. Never fully trust an intellectual who inspires a book called *What Freud Really Meant*.)

Freud's complicated theories explain what is happening, but we still don't understand why some men feel compelled to go down this path. Another of Freud's theories concerns the Oedipus complex, where boys in early childhood want to possess their mother and kill their father. This occurs in the 'phallic' stage of sexual development, when boys become aware of gender differences and see their father as a rival for their mother. This rivalry fuels a castration anxiety in the developing child, which occurs when the young male child first sees the female genitalia. He presumes the lack of a penis is due to castration and, in the Oedipal phase, the boy fears castration by his father. Part of normal adult development is the resolution of this anxiety by maturation. If the process is interrupted by dysfunctional parenting then the child is prone to developing one or more perversions, of which the paraphilias are an example. I should add at this point that Freud's theories, although an important contribution to the debate, are not widely held among the modern psychotherapeutic community.

Kurt Freund, a Canadian physician, thought the paraphilias were disorders of the courtship ritual, which he believed had four stages:

1. Looking for and appraising potential partners
2. Non tactile contact – smiling and talking with someone
3. Tactile contact, like kissing or petting
4. Consensual sexual intercourse

The paraphilias arise from abnormalities at each stage of this process. So, voyeurism is an abnormality of stage 1; exhibitionism, stage 2; frotteurism stage 3; and biastophilia or paraphilic rape, a disturbance of stage 4. Freund also invented penile plesthysmography, a scientific means of measuring a man's reaction to certain erotic stimuli, an important method of identifying sexual abnormalities.

The role of the mother in the history of exhibitionism is developed by the British author Alex Legray in his book *Exhibitionism and other Sex Aberrations*. This was published in 1969 and has a slightly racy feel to it – the front cover has not a flasher, but a naked woman whipping a man. The back of the book is full of adverts for other 'specialist' publications – *The Astrology of Sex*, *The Sex Jungle*, *The Encyclopaedia of Sex Worship* and so on, which at the time meant pornography dressed up as academic literature. There is, however, an attempt to put an academic veneer on the issue and it probably does give an accurate impression of the views of the time.

Legray does not mince his words. The primary cause of male genital exhibitionism is the mother: 'She is responsible ... for giving the boy a complex about his appearance and his body, most particularly about his genitals. This is brought about by the sometimes evil and sexually perverse manner in which fond mothers display their young sons to friends and relatives, mostly, if not always, of the female sex.' It was quite normal, Legray continued, for the male child to be paraded in front of women, 'naked, or nearly so', so he develops a connection between his nakedness and the presence of women. The exhibitionist, therefore, is not born but made by the females of his family. It is nurture, not nature, and when he reaches adulthood he tries to recreate those moments of which he was, 'dimly aware of a certain sort of thrill.' This is compounded by the fact that, 'every male is narcissistic at heart'. Eventually it becomes the main source of sexual excitement and orgasm becomes impossible unless exhibitionistic scenes are being acted out. Alex Legray quotes the true story of an exhibitionist, a 'Mr Y' from Peter Capon's book *The Sex Jungle*:

> Mr Y was a compulsive exhibitionist who, although married, could not resist the temptation to travel out into the country in his car searching for quiet spots where he knew young girls would pass. He would spend hours in a state of tension, waiting for the sound of young girls walking down a path that would lead by where he was hiding. As soon as he saw females on the way he would be compelled, with trembling hands, to disrobe himself and to be engaged in masturbating when they passed by where he was standing. This he achieved practically every time he went on these excursions, and he confessed to getting far more pleasure in this act than he did in any act of normal intercourse with his wife.

The piece concludes with Mr Y's own confession:

> The act of knowing that a girl, or a couple of girls, would come across me naked from the waist down and sexually excited thrills me beyond anything. Whether they are frightened, or disgusted, or amused does not matter ... there have been times when a couple of coarse girls have actually stopped and watched me, with evident interest, complete my actions. This has been the supreme mo-

ment for me and such a circumstance has lived with me for a long time afterwards.

I am afraid I am quite amoral where this sort of thing is concerned. I am not able to think of possible conse-quences while I am doing it. Neither am I able to think of what harm I am doing the girls. I am compelled by a force quite beyond my control to expose myself – to enjoy every moment of the situation – whatever hap-pens to be the reactions of the girls. After it is all over, my one thought is to get dressed and to escape in the car. Strangely, I seem to have been doing this on and off ever since I first became able to express myself sexually. I am happily married but I do not enjoy intercourse with my wife ... I can honestly say that the only time I am able to get a proper orgasm is by showing off in this way to a girl or group of girls. I know I will get into serious trouble one day but until that day comes I see no way of overcoming this habit.

From the studies of exhibitionists this would seem to be a fairly typical case. You will note he is the type 2 exhibitionist charac-terised by active masturbation, repeat offending and lack of remorse. He is also compelled to do it, describing himself as in the grip of uncontrollable forces. Alex Legray thought exhibi-tionists were by nature lonely men, often with aggressive wives or mothers who could not face up to adult sexual activity and sought refuge in childhood fantasies.

Exhibitionism as a reaction to castration anxiety was explored by the psychologist Jeno Harvik, among others, one of whom (Sandor Lorand, a Hungarian psychoanalyst) also thought that exhibitionists had a fear of the *vagina dentate,* the vagina with teeth. Others believed that exhibitionists suffered from colophobia, a fear of the vagina.

The reasons, therefore, for exhibitionism are varied but coa-lesce around the following theories: it is a result of dysfunctional parenting, notably maternal; it is a personality disorder; it is a defence against predatory females; it is an indication of deeper psychiatric issues; it is a sign of a narcissistic immaturity; and finally, that it is a masochistic act that invites shame and disgrace. The cause in most men is, as the medical profession would say, multifactorial; that is, no single cause predominates.

One of the aforementioned psychotherapists, Jano Harnik, also looked at female genital exhibitionism. This is much rarer than male exhibitionism, which Harnik thought was down to Freud's theory of female 'penis envy'. This is the adolescent female equivalent of the male castration anxiety when the female in the phallic stage of development realises that she doesn't have a penis and competes with her mother for the attention of the father (the Electra complex). Harnik thought this lack of a penis meant there was nothing for the female to expose, which is why there are fewer female genital exhibitionists than male. He did not, however, believe women in general did not indulge in exhibitionism, but that it took a different form – the display of the whole body. Not necessarily in nudity, but in general appearance, using dress and makeup and mannerisms to exhibitionist effect.

It would certainly appear that there is something fundamentally different in the male and female attitudes to exhibitionism. The case histories for male acts of indecent exposure are extensive, whereas female genital exhibitionism is extremely rare. In fact it was so infrequent that it was possible up until the 1960s to state that it didn't exist. And up to that point, it was probably true. The fact that it has changed, not just as far as exposure is concerned, but in the whole issue of a woman's role in society, is one of the most interesting aspects of modern exhibitionism.

If prehistoric societies, and even the old Anglo Saxon society of Dark Age Britain, had female genital exposure as part of a ritual or display, that was all in the past. The last period of licentiousness in Britain was the Regency, and even if there had been a brief wobble in the 1920s, British society in the early 1960s was generally straight-laced. Women dressed conservatively and were usually housewives and mothers in a male-dominated society. There were unwritten rules as to how women should behave – don't flirt, don't dress provocatively, look after the children, and obey your husband in every respect. These were the boundaries of a religious society, the religion, of course, being interpreted and administered almost solely by men.

This is not to say that we had an entirely moral society. All sorts went on behind closed doors in prim and proper Britain, notably among the more 'racy' sets in theatrical and aristocratic circles. There was prostitution, striptease and dirty magazines, but they existed in a sort of closed world which never imposed upon ordinary people. It was a very *moral* world, where people were genuinely shocked and upset by things like adultery. I remember hearing vague rumours (that was all they were, because these things were never discussed in front of the children) that someone we knew had moved away because she had been having an affair. And that was the point, if you were found out it was the end, socially, in post-war Britain.

Then the boundaries changed, staring with the role of women in society. For a start, they looked different as the fashion world, inspired by Mary Quant's miniskirt, targeted teenage women. And the push began for equality and liberation with charismatic figures like Germaine Greer natural material for the burgeoning broadcast media. More and more of the female body became exposed by fashion, much to the disgust of the more traditional elements of society. Unfortunately for them, the 'swinging sixties' had infiltrated the mainstream media, which became less deferential to the powers that be. Up until the 1960s there was an unspoken code of behaviour between newspaper editors and the Establishment about certain matters that should not be published, like the private antics of public figures. In the sixties all that changed and a more aggressive press revealed the truth about power, exposing the Profumo affair and other scandals. (It is interesting to think that arguably our greatest Prime Minister, Churchill, would not have survived in today's world if details of his alcohol consumption had become known.) An increasingly liberal society decriminalised abortion and homosexuality, acknowledging their place in a tolerant society.

For women this meant emancipation, the benefits of which included the freedom to behave differently. It became more acceptable for women to have a career, and then to continue their career after they had children. To my father's generation, and every generation as far back as you can go, this would have been unthinkable. That was only fifty years ago, which is astonishing if you think about it. (And, in a sort of weird twist, it is now *only* possible for most families to own homes if both partners work; what the right wing would call the triumph of liberal capitalism.)

The increasing social liberalisation saw the previously taboo enter the mainstream. Images of partially clothed and naked women became more commonplace, even if they were tucked away on the top shelf of the newsagents. The watershed event, however, occurred on 17 November 1970 when *The Sun* newspaper published its first topless Page 3 girl. This was a crucial event in the history of female exhibitionism as the naked female image, previously either unobtainable, or furtive, or lustful, suddenly became commonplace. Something men had desired for centuries was now available in a newspaper and surrounded by stories not of lust but financial crises, natural disasters and petty crime. The naked female form has always attracted the tacky and the sordid, but this was something else: humdrum nudity, everyday nudity, nothing special. (Try saying 'liberation' like a balloon deflating.)

The Page 3 girl was a landmark in the history of female exhibitionism, and the next occurred in the unlikely surroundings of Twickenham Rugby Football ground on 2 January 1982. England were playing Australia when a tense game was interrupted by the figure of Erica Roe streaking topless across the pitch. The image, as they say, 'went global', managing to legitimise female nudity and make a feminist statement at the same time. Up until then, streaking had been the preserve of young men and like most male nudity was regarded as vulgar or obscene, and certainly not erotic. A young woman going topless is a different experience altogether, and is still fairly frequently seen at public events like music festivals.

The naked female form has now entered mainstream culture, being used widely throughout the world of the arts in all its forms, not just in tastefully executed oil paintings. It is also used in the commercial world as an advertising tool, usually stopping short of full nudity while conveying an explicitly erotic message. More fundamentally, the real revolution in female exhibitionism is in its relationship to pornography. Pornography has been with us as long as the printing press and in England, especially, was subject to censorship, the first Obscene Publication Act being passed in 1857. Again, although it has been around as long as civilisation in one form or another, it was until recently very much a furtive pursuit, confined to the top shelves of newsagents and grubby little theatres in Soho. It reeked of shame and disgrace, and was always something to be kept hidden. In the 1950s and early 1960s, no girl in her right mind would admit to being a topless model or pornographic actress. The only ones who did were probably trapped in the murky world of metropolitan vice, excluded from what was known as 'polite society'. There were no stars and no real names in the pornography of the 1940s and 1950s.

The film that changed everything was the 1972 movie *Deep Throat*, starring Linda Lovelace. Although not the first mainstream 'adult' movie, it became the most notorious and made Linda Lovelace a star. The key to the film's impact lay in the fact that it was a story, not just a series of sex scenes, so it required a modicum of acting talent. It meant that Linda Lovelace could be regarded as an actress, and if she was not respectable, then she was at least accepted as an 'artist'.

The 1970s saw the adult movie industry establish itself in the USA and, more importantly for the story of female exhibitionism, the rise of the named porn actress. The numbers involved are astonishing: in the 1960s there were only four named stars; by the end of the 1970s this had risen to over forty. By the 1980s this had risen to nearly 100, the 1990s 150, and in the 2000s an astonishing 500. Although many work under pseudonyms, their biographies are readily accessible on the internet, and being named is clearly important to establishing themselves as a 'brand' (of which more in the next chapter).

Like any business, the industry has annual awards ceremony, the *Adult Video News* (AVN) Awards, not conducted in some seamy backstreet dive but in a major venue, with all the glitz and glamour of a small-scale Oscars. To win an award is clearly a major honour, with plenty of competition. Like the Oscars, the *Adult Video News* Awards has various categories in the competition. There is a Best Film, Best Actress, Best Actor, and so on, just like the standard film ceremonies. There are also awards for individual scenes, like Best Group Sex or Best Oral Sex scene, even down to Most Outrageous Sex Scene (won in 2009 by *Night of the Giving Head*, in case you're interested). The list is fairly comprehensive and covers every possible variation on the theme, including many that were once considered illegal, like sodomy.

It is at this point in the story you have to take stock. What we are dealing with here is exhibitionism at its most outrageous, the open exaltation of sex in public. Forty years ago this would have been social suicide, yet now it is inching its way towards respectability. If you take away the actual acts themselves, what you have is a standard entertainment business plan. The actresses talk about it in an almost matter-of-fact way, with advice to aspiring stars like, 'don't do anything on screen that you haven't tried in private,' or, 'keep fit and avoid drugs'. There are health plans, testing for sexually transmitted diseases and even a code of practice. And there is the goal of making it in the mainstream movie business, like Sasha Grey, a porn actress cast in Stephen Sondheim's film *The Girlfriend Experience*.

The growth in pornography has mirrored the rise of broadcast media. Initially it was accessed almost exclusively by adult males, but that has changed with the rise of the internet. According to *Best Internet Software Review,* an online research organisation, there are nearly 30,000 users per second worldwide who are accessing pornography sites. An astonishing one in three of these are claimed to be women. The industry generated over 20 billion dollars in revenue in 2006 alone.

Or did it? According to *Forbes* magazine, estimates of internet pornography usage are wildly exaggerated, especially in terms of the revenue it generates. Most experts see porn sites as languishing a long way behind news sites, finance sites and even greeting card websites with regard to the number of hits. In terms of global internet traffic it is still a relatively minor player. What the internet has done is to increase both the number and range of users. There is a world of difference between going into a newsagent and publicly buying a magazine, and clicking on a porn site in the privacy of your own home. And the consumers, once almost exclusively men, are now being joined by women and, more alarmingly, children. I would guess most children leaving mainstream British schools will at least know of the existence of pornography sites and will almost certainly have seen some, probably on a mobile phone. Counselling services dealing with addictions, which 'cybersex' is claimed to be, are reporting an increase in the number of women, especially young women, seeking help. In some circles, it would appear, pornography is socially acceptable – a sea change in public morality.

This, I think, is another landmark in the history of sexual exhibitionism. There is not enough information yet to see where exactly this is going, but it may be that we are about to fundamentally change our attitude to genital exposure. In less than twenty years, centuries of morality have been discarded in favour of an 'anything goes' approach. The internet is moving so fast that traditional structures of power and authority cannot keep up. Censorship laws, designed among other things to protect the public have, virtually overnight, become meaningless. What does that mean for a society, who might wish to retain some sense of value and propriety? If you can take something like pornography, strip away its morality and simply send it out there as a commodity, what sort of a society are you going to get? I am afraid I don't know, but the legitimate side of exhibitionism – artistic performance – may contain some clues. If we take exhibitionism as public display, and add in egotism, greed, theft, snobbery, double dealing, and vast amounts of money, you get a recognisable human activity which could act as a parable for our times. Welcome to the world of art.

4

Exhibitionism as public display 1: representational art

Drawing, painting and sculpture are some of mankind's oldest activities, dating back 30,000 years to the Upper Palaeolithic period of the Stone Age. The most famous paintings are found in the Lascaux caves in southern France, where the walls are decorated with pictures of animals and hunters. The signature work is in a cave called the Hall of Bulls where bulls, horses and stags are depicted in a mural, the largest bull being 17 feet long.

Tempting though it may be to see this as the work of the first 'artists' to seek public acclaim through performance, we cannot say this for certain because we do not know why they were painted. It is possible that they were the work of the world's first commercial artist, someone who painted in return for food or clothing. It could be, too, that they were done simply for aesthetic pleasure. What is more likely is that they fulfilled some spiritual function, either relating a myth, or fixing an image, as part of a hunting ritual.

They were certainly not designed to be seen by large numbers of people, being hidden deep in the cave complex. Their inaccessibility meant they lay undiscovered until 1940 when four French teenagers, led by 18-year-old Marcel Radivat, found the long entrance tunnel which led to the paintings.

They were opened to the public in 1948, but almost immediately began to decay because of the carbon dioxide produced by visitors. They were clearly painted for a reason, yet their survival implies they remained largely unseen. Modern artists want their work to be widely accessed, yet the Palaeolithic painter appears to have deliberately hidden his or her work away. Perhaps they did this because other paintings nearer the mouth of caves rapidly deteriorated. It is also possible that viewing the paintings was part of some religious rite and access was strictly controlled by a primitive priestly caste. Whatever the reason, from the very first stirrings of the artistic spirit we find not every picture on a wall is what it seems. Representative art begins in ambiguity.

This may seem a curious way in which to start a story about art as exhibitionism, but the closer you get to the subject you realise how complicated it has become. For the uninitiated it all seems relatively straightforward. The artist puts their talent into creating a work of art, and then sends it into the public domain. There it receives both a monetary and artistic value, and if people like it, they will say so, and possibly even buy it. If it is really good then the creator becomes internationally famous and hailed as a genius. Whatever the extent of their talent, it seems axiomatic that an artist needs to exhibit their work to be appreciated.

The art on the walls of Lascaux tell us a different story, however, one which runs right through the story of art to the present day. To go back to the actual composition of the work, I remember visiting a prehistoric painted cave in Southern France (not Lascaux), and walking around just taking in the images. Without any prior knowledge they soon become familiar, unremarkable even, as one ochre animal succeeds another. You are in awe of their age, but without any hinterland they quickly pale as works of art. Yet as soon as their back story is filled in – how they were painted, why they were painted and, most importantly, what they may represent – they cease to be mere arrangements of colours but become something vibrant and fascinating. A work of art can be taken at face value, but it can only be understood when one considers the circumstances behind its creation.

If that makes prehistoric art something beyond its simple appearance, then where does it leave modern art, which has centuries of tradition behind it? A painting by a famous artist hanging in a gallery would appear to most of us to be a straightforward case of exhibitionism as public display. The artist is the exhibitionist, and the picture is the exhibit. And yet, this is merely the tip of the iceberg. The identity of the artist is obviously of paramount importance, especially when one is looking at the work as a saleable commodity. The technical skill of the work is an indication of value, although it is not nearly as important as the name of the artist – a painting by a forger may be identical to the original, but once it is realised as such it ceases to have the same market value. Where the painting sits in the canon of art, both present and historical is vital. For a work by a dead artist its provenance, or where it came from, is essential, as is the period when it was created. If you take public recognition as a measure of successful exhibitionism, then where it is displayed is crucial. A painting hanging in the Tate will be seen by hundreds of thousands, whereas only a fraction of that number will see a work in a small seaside gallery. Challenging work that requires interpretation needs critics and historians. Museum curators, the creators of exhibitions, dictate the presentation and interpretation of high art. In the world of international art, auction houses, galleries and the identity of the collector feed the importance and value of the exhibit. And finally, the purchasers of expensive art are locked in a small but competitive world where huge amounts of money are chasing a finite number of objects, to the extent where the actual composition of the work of art becomes almost irrelevant. The artist is no longer the sole exhibitionist, nor the work of art the only thing that is being exhibited.

To understand how the hinterland around a work of art became so complicated, we need to work through the various meanings of art through the centuries. Ancient Egypt was the first civilisation to leave an extensive pictorial record of its culture, using hieroglyphs as writing and decorating their tombs with fabulous pictures, statues and sarcophagi. Yet their purpose was very different from what we understand today as the purpose of art. They were not looked at solely to be admired, but as something to be understood. The hieroglyphs had a purpose, to tell a story, or to impart information. Because the images were so strange, it wasn't until the finding of the Rosetta Stone, two thousand years later, that the script was deciphered, and then it was decades before anyone could 'read' the hieroglyphs confidently. Even now, when the images have passed into mainstream culture, the strange gods of Ancient Egypt, with their human bodies and animal heads, still appear otherworldly. From a technical point of view they are flat and two dimensional, although their art does begin to flow in later dynasties. Similarly the uncannily lifelike sarcophagi and statues were not just a tribute to the skill of the artist, but were deliberately made to ensure the reincarnation of the individual. Tutankhamen's sarcophagus *had* to be a lifelike copy in order to receive his soul. The use of gold and precious stones were not just decorative, although that may have been part of their purpose, but necessary to prove the status of the pharaoh. They were beautiful to look at, but their *raison d'etre* was to provide the god-king with an environment suitable for his reincarnation. One of the most enduring links in the history of human endeavour, the relationship between art and spirituality, began with the earliest forms of artistic representation.

While Egypt was flourishing, Europe was a barbarian backwater, with one single exception. On the island of Crete, the Minoans created the first recognisable European art with pottery, statues and painted frescoes. The figures depicted are very human and far removed from the bird and jackal gods of Egypt, and clearly influence the founders of European civilisation as we know it, the Ancient Greeks. And here we are on surer ground.

Greek civilisation developed between 750BC and roughly 150BC, and was divided into three periods: the Archaic, from 750 to 500BC; the Classical, from 500 to 336BC; and the Hellenistic, from 336 to 146BC. This was perhaps the most astonishing 600 years in human history. During this time the foundations of intellectual activity were laid down, ranging from mathematics and philosophy to architecture and drama. Most importantly for the story of art, Ancient Greece saw sculpture and painting evolve from the purely symbolic to a thing of beauty in its own right.

It is impossible to overestimate the importance of this transition. During this brief time in human history three very important developments in representative art take shape. The first was the transformation of the human form from the stiff and formal figures of Egyptian art into something vibrant. Greek statuary was especially impressive, using flowing lines and active poses to indicate movement. In painting, the Greeks developed foreshortening to give perspective, which was one of the great innovations in the history of art. The Greeks may have been making images of Gods, but they looked like real people.

The second great gift of the Greeks to the world of art was the identity of the artists. We know the names of some of the great sculptors – Pheidias, Myron, Praxiteles and Lysippus. These were real people, names verifiable from other sources. Although we do know that artists and sculptors were not particularly highly regarded in Ancient Greece, being regarded as artisans rather than creative geniuses, it still gives us the link between the work and the artist.

As the art developed, it began to lose its roots in magic and religion, and became something to be created for its own sake and to promote the identity of the artist. In the Greek and Roman era, spanning the birth of Christ, the status of artists improved and their lives became worthy of examination and biography. As none of the painted works have survived, it is only through the written descriptions of the works that we can trace the great advances the Greeks made in the technical aspects of artistic composition, using light, shade and perspective among other things. I think of it as a time close to our own, when dramatic innovations in style and composition produced 'collectable' artists.

And this was the third gift, if you like. Works of art became commodities, to be bought and sold, a desirable object which could increase in value. To own a famous work of art was a means of displaying one's wealth. The relationship between art and money had begun, as had the relationship between public display and status. The rich Greek or Roman saw the ownership of beautiful objects in much the same way as we do, or rather, they gave us the values, which are still relevant today. Having talent as an artist was a means of earning money, and being rich meant you could afford to buy art. Outbidding a rival was not simply a desire to own a work of art, but a means of signalling one's superiority. The complexities of artistic exhibitionism were becoming apparent.

The Christianisation of the Roman Empire saw a fundamental change in the purpose of art as public display. The fourth of the Ten Commandments forbade the worship of graven images, which led to many statues being destroyed. Paintings and frescoes, however, were a different matter. Gregory the Great, who was Pope between AD590 and 604, believed that the mainly illiterate population understood Biblical events better when they were portrayed in pictorial form. This began a long tradition of religious frescoes and icons, painted in a style simple to understand by anonymous artists. The work was exhibited, put on public display, but its purpose was instructive, to bring the viewer closer to God. Although this meant the early basilicas were often splendidly decorated, that was not the art's primary function, nor was fame the artist's creative impulse. It became rather like the artists in the East, whose purpose was to faithfully reproduce classical themes with little or no deviation from a standard pattern.

Western art, though, was always different, even in the Dark Ages when the church was left as the only repository of high art. The barbarians outside the monasteries and abbeys were producing vivid art of their own, and this was primarily decorative. The fabulous interweaving shapes and animals of Saxon and Celtic art found its way into the inscribed bibles of the monasteries, resulting in works like the Lindisfarne Gospels, produced under the guidance of the monk Eadfrith. The images displayed in the monasteries and churches developed slowly until the time of Giotto, who began painting more lifelike images. We are inching towards the time when the world of art changed forever, the burst of creativity known as the Renaissance.

To list all the various masters is beyond the scope of this short chapter, but it is in the artistic crucible of fifteenth-century Italy that high art, both practical and intellectual, was formed. Great artists like Michelangelo and Leonardo da Vinci produced fabulous works, bringing new techniques to painting and sculpture which breathed life into their creations, and initiating the continuous revolution in style which has endured to the present day. The masters had their studios, training apprentices in their style and using them to paint parts of their masterworks. The hinterland around art developed with patrons, the Catholic Church and wealthy nobles, financing the careers of artists. The Medici family of Florence commissioned one of the world's most famous paintings, Botticelli's 'Venus'. It was said that the Medici's bought art to help 'cleanse' their money, some of which had been obtained through usury, or moneylending, which still had the taint of the New Testament. (Jesus drove the money lenders and 'pigeon sellers' out of the temple.)

Most importantly, a work of art was now regarded as a thing of beauty in its own right, regardless of its subject matter. Although the work may contain a story, or clues to a story, the technical skill and composition of the work now gave it both artistic and financial merit. To own a work by a master added beauty and refinement to one's home, as well as being a not-so-subtle hint as to one's status. So, an artist needed public display to get recognised, and the wealthy patron or buyer enjoyed exhibiting the work to reflect their taste and buying power. Either way, both had exhibited their exalted status.

Prior to Leonardo and Michelangelo, painters and sculptors were still regarded as artisans whose skill was admired, but who were not thought to be creative artists of the first rank. All that changed in the wake of the great masters, whose genius was recognised wherever it was exhibited. Leonardo and Michelangelo were polymaths of the highest order, whose inquiring minds stretched far beyond the world of art. From this point on the painter and sculptor received due acclaim for their talent, elevating these two forms of art to the pedestal occupied by theatre and poetry.

We also begin to learn a little more about the artists themselves. Michelangelo was a solitary man, prone to melancholy, who never married. Leonardo was physically beautiful, charming and gracious, and a naturally gentle man. The sexuality of both of them has been the subject of much speculation, but their discreet natures meant that very little can be said for certain. They were both private men.

An artist who came along a bit later, Caravaggio, was a completely different character. He changed the way people were portrayed, painting with a stark naturalism that is almost photographic in its detail. His life, however, was full of torment. He killed a man and had to flee Rome, and lived a life of brawling and excess until he died of a fever at the early age of thirty-eight. We are beginning to see the link between genius and mental instability that weaves through the lives of many artists.

The fourteenth century was a watershed in the history of art, when the Italian Renaissance saw an astonishing number of great artists flourish in Florence, Rome and Venice. But great art was not confined to Italy. The Netherlands already had a reputation for innovative painting through artists like van

Eyck, and the Renaissance sparked a similar creative surge in Northern Europe. The pantheon of great artists is beginning to assemble, with Titian, Rafael, Giorgione, van der Weyden, Rembrandt, Dürer, among many others, achieving fame. If art before the fourteenth century was confined to a few religious artists who sought neither fame nor riches, then the Renaissance threw open the doors and eventually created the world of art as we know it today.

By the sixteenth and seventeenth centuries, the subject matter was becoming more varied, veering away from the strictly religious nature of most early Middle Ages painting, although the Catholic Church remained one of the most powerful patrons of art. The real change, however, was in the society outside the artist's studio. The growth of international trade and the rise of the capitalist society saw the traditional sources of wealth and power shift, from the Church and Aristocracy to the newly rich mercantile class. There had long been a limited market for art, but as Europe got richer, so the demand for art increased.

One of the first collectors of art was King Charles I, who assembled an impressive collection of the signature works of his time, including paintings by Rembrandt and Rafael. The early seventeenth century saw the creation of the art market, where paintings were put up for sale with a value attached. A 'great auction of pictures' from the collection of Lord Melford was held in London in 1693, the first documented sale of works of art. The following century saw the sale of art become more widespread, laying the foundations for the modern, highly competitive and viscerally exciting business of selling beauty. The sale of the collection of the Earl of Oxford in 1741 attracted representations from the wealthiest in the land, including Walpole, the Prime Minister. A van Dyke portrait sold for 165 guineas, a considerable sum for the time.

The growing market for art saw the establishment of auction houses, the most famous being Sotheby's, founded in 1744, and Christie's, in 1766. Auctions created a dramatic competitive atmosphere, in its way becoming a form of entertainment in its own right. A great auction is live theatre as a sporting event, with the auctioneer as both a performer and referee, the crowd as the act. It is entertainment, pure and simple, even in the rarefied atmosphere of Christie's and Sotheby's, where the staff have uniforms and white gloves, and the exhibition of financial power is coated in honeyed refinement. By the end of the Victorian era, the commercial side of art was as much a form of public display as the art itself.

But we are running ahead of ourselves. The next great event in the story of art after the Renaissance was the Reformation, which was a Northern European phenomenon. Its importance lay in the Protestant antipathy to religious imagery, which saw paintings and statues from our churches and monasteries looted and destroyed. This anti-exhibitionism saw virtually all of England's art disappear, and it reminds us that public display has a negative side. The spirit behind the destruction was, paradoxically, positive, because Protestants believed that the road to God had been cluttered with images of saints and they needed to be removed to purify their faith. For artists it meant religious subjects were off limits and they had to find new subjects to paint and sculpt. This in turn led to the era of the great portrait painters, led in England by the Flemish artists van Dyke and Rubens. So we are beginning to get the emergence of the artist as someone who not only has to paint, but sell themselves and their pictures.

The next great event was the French Revolution, which the art historian E. H. Gombrich thinks acts as a line in the sand, separating the world of the Old Masters from nineteenth- and twentieth-century art. The old market for art, confined to the rich or the church, was destroyed. Paris became the hotbed for the rapidly changing world of art and artists began to grow their hair and dress expressively, in the manner we think of today.

More importantly, the nineteenth century French artists looked at the world differently and dramatically changed the world of portraiture, both landscape and figurative. They gave us Realism with painters like Millet and Courbet portraying scenes from ordinary life, shocking the art world with pictures of peasants or the painters themselves in casual dress. But that was mild compared to what came next. Here is a quote from a press review of an exhibition held in Paris in 1876:

> The Rue le Peletier is a road of disasters. After the fire at the Opera, there is now another disaster there. An exhibition has just been opened ... which allegedly contains paintings. I enter and my horrified eyes behold something terrible. Five or six lunatics ... have exhibited their works. These would-be artists call themselves revolutionaries. They take a piece of canvas, dab a few patches of paint on it at random, and sign the whole thing with their name. It is a delusion of the same kind as if the inmates of Bedlam picked up stones from the wayside and imagined that they had found diamonds.

These 'lunatics' who had toyed with the stones of Bedlam were the Impressionists, among them Manet and Monet. The genius of the Impressionists was to realise that the human eye and brain can formulate an image from visual clues, without necessarily needing every detail to be exact. They captured the essence of a subject with a few short brush strokes and paid particular attention to the way light played on their subjects.

From the point of view of exhibitionism and public display, what happened then was of the upmost importance. This group of artists were challenging the public perception of what constituted art. They were displaying something radical and offering a new way of looking at the world. They were displaying their artistic genius, but at the same time opening a window into a new world. This was exhibitionism both as public display and as a milestone in human artistic progress.

The Impressionists were followed by van Gogh, Gauguin and Cézanne who, in turn, revolutionised art by eschewing complex techniques and returning to a simpler style. All three worked without any hope of fame or reward, and were solitary men. The pursuit of what they saw as artistic truth came at a price – Gauguin attempted suicide, while van Gogh cut off his ear in a brothel and, it is widely suspected, took his own life. Artists of all disciplines have a higher rate of mental illness than the general public, and there does seem a link between mental dysfunction and creativity. Van Gogh, had bursts of creativity which would fit with a manic-depressive personality, where the sufferer veers between manic, active, highs and dreadful, pointless, lows. Mental illness aside, 'artists' in general were beginning to exist outside of polite society. The exhibitionist personality, if there is such a thing, exists in the borderland between normality and mental disorder.

Most of the artists we now consider famous exhibited in the Salon des Refusees, a Paris gallery which took works rejected by the Paris Salon, the official showcase of the Beaux Arts in France. The Salon was founded in 1725, and from the mid-1700s to the end of the 1800s was the world's most prestigious artistic establishment. The catalogues of their exhibitions are important historical documents in their own right, while the descriptions of the paintings saw the genesis of the art critic. It is entirely typical of the complexities in the world of art that the paintings which we now consider masterpieces, like the work of the Impressionists, were rejected by the Salon. And not just rejected – the debate was heated and personal, with those great names vilified as talentless frauds.

In Britain, the Royal Academy of Arts was founded in 1768, and although its history is not as tempestuous as the Salon, it was until recently thought to be the home of the 'Establishment' view of art. Like the Salon, it was seen to favour traditional styles and compositions of paintings, rather than anything new or edgy. Although considered somewhat grand, the Royal Academy is actually run by eighty practising artists who must be elected, one of the most recent being Tracey Emin.

The nineteenth century saw the mushrooming of outlets for the display of art, many of them started as charitable enterprises. Probably the most famous in Britain are the Tate galleries and the National Gallery. But there are hundreds more worldwide, certainly at least one major exhibition centre in every Western city. And although they are 'stand-alone', and often just reflect a variety of local works or the collections of local benefactors, those in major cities will be in the market for new acquisitions. Exhibitionism in its literal sense is a competitive activity.

As we get closer to the present day, we get to know more about the personality of artists, and as we have seen, some led lives unbound by conventional morals. But their lives were essentially conventional in that they attempted to paint what they could see. The twentieth century saw the formal concept of art turned on its head by the revolutionary artistic movements around the turn of the century and the First World War, of which the best known is Surrealism. The essence of Surrealism was its unexpectedness – the combination of unsettling images, the mixture of the exotic and the commonplace, and the bizarre associations between images. The theories of Sigmund Freud, who explored the unconscious and the significance of dreams, were a major influence on the Surrealists. The leader of the movement, André Breton, believed that the work was merely symbolic of a revolutionary philosophy – in other words the work of art was a connection to a much wider community not contained within any particular political or cultural grouping.

The most famous Surrealist painter is probably Salvador Dali, and the reason he is best known is because he took the Surrealist philosophy into his life. He dressed extravagantly in a long cape, sporting a waxed moustache, and twirling a cane. He took to travelling with a pet ocelot and appeared in one gallery in a diving suit. Images of him are almost always exhibitionist in the sense that they convey extravagant behaviour and imply controversy, of which there was plenty in his life. He was expelled from the Surrealists because of his apparent sympathy with fascism, and excoriated by George Orwell for his childish desire to shock. Dali and the other Surrealists were not just creating a surreal work of art, they were trying to lead a surreal life. This idea of the artist as someone who had not just broken the conventions of their art, but sought to exhibit a different attitude to society, resonates throughout the twentieth century.

The break with the past was emphasised by the new directions representative art was embracing. The painted image was reinvented with styles like Cubism and Minimalism, or did away with traditional imagery altogether, as in abstract art. Artists like Jackson Pollock also rejected conventional painting techniques, abandoning the traditional easel and brush, and dripping or smearing paint on canvas. Picasso used Cubism to reinvent the human form, while the Italian Futurists used images of technology like the car to suggest speed and violence. The Rive Gauche, or left bank, of the River Seine in Paris hosted a community of artists and writers including Picasso, Matisse, Rimbaud and Hemingway, who changed the direction of their chosen art form.

The traditional function of the artist to create visual objects capable of instant appreciation by the observer was in turn challenged by the French artist Marcel Duchamp, who worked in the early part of the twentieth century. In an art world still dominated by painting, however revolutionary, he sent a strange piece to an exhibition in 1917. It was a factory made urinal, nothing more, with the name 'R. Mutt' sloppily painted on the side. Duchamp called it 'Fountain'. The reaction of the art world in 1917, unsurprisingly, was one of contempt mixed with outright hostility. The work was removed from the exhibition. The artist was a disciple of Dadaism, a revolutionary precursor of Surrealism, which rejected traditional artistic merit and promoted the non-aesthetic, the illogical and the transient. Duchamp explained his philosophy thus:

> The creative act is not performed by the artist alone; the spectator brings the work into contact with the external world by deciphering and interpreting its inner qualifications, and thus adds his contribution to the creative act.

Now this, I would suggest, is a truly revolutionary concept. The work of art now becomes not just the piece itself, but the images and concepts formed by everyone who has viewed the work of art. The purpose of exhibiting the work is not just to put it on public display, but to amplify the work in the collective conscience. 'Fountain' was voted the most influential twentieth century work of art by a panel of critics in 2004.

All these various movements are fine in themselves, but professional artists still had to find a way to live. There is every point in producing work which stretches the boundaries of art, but most of this is anathema to the traditional art institutions and way beyond the comprehension of the general public. So the artist is in a quandary. What is the point of producing ground-breaking work if it won't sell and you cannot make enough money to continue painting? There are plenty of examples of artists who suffered rejection in their lifetime and died in poverty – van Gogh, Gauguin, Monet, Cézanne and Toulouse-Lautrec, among many others. In the early 1900s, not only did the direction of art change, but so did the people who bought it. Enter the Collector.

From the Renaissance onwards, the rich and powerful have always collected art, and patronised promising artists. Mostly they collected established works or sponsored traditional artists. The twentieth century, however, saw the rise of a different type of collector, one who wasn't afraid to support new and challenging art. Very often they came from mercantile backgrounds and were commonly born into riches with the time and money to indulge their passion. One of the most famous was Peggy Guggenheim, a bohemian heiress who travelled extensively in Europe and built a collection of modern art under the guidance of the English critic Herbert Read. She had opened a gallery in London, which ran at a loss, before deciding – on the advice of Read – to buy modern art. She left for Paris with a regime to 'buy at least one painting a day'. When she returned from scouring France she had acquired ten Picassos, forty Ernsts, eight Mirós, four Magrittes, three Dalis and three Man Rays, among others. This must count as one of the greatest shopping expeditions of all time.

She was not alone. Other famous collectors included Bernard Arnault, a French billionaire, Eli Broad, Walter Chrysler, David Rockefeller and Guy de Rothschild. Collecting art became a favourite way of displaying one's wealth. It was also an exhibition of the collector's taste and power, for if word got out that a particular collector was investing in a new artist, then the artist was elevated to superstar status (you can tell we're in the twentieth century). In the modern world, Charles Saatchi, David Geffen and the Qatari Royal Family are among the best known collectors.

Surrounding the artist and the collector was an expanding hinterland of art critics, gallery owners and art experts. The list of famous art critics runs to nearly 80 names, some of whom, like the Americans Clement Greenberg, Leo Steinberg and Harold Rosenberg, had a huge influence in the world of the arts. The American writer Tom Wolfe dubbed them the 'Kings of Cultureberg.'

'Cultureberg' is a good way to describe the world of the arts in the twentieth century; a community walled off from the rest of the world. Consumer capitalism was rapidly changing the way people lived, and the rise of broadcast media introduced the concept of mass consumer culture, with the airways pumping out light entertainment, and Constable's 'The Hay Wain' decorating tins of biscuits. The producers of mass culture were not above using psychological techniques to increase consumption, a rather sinister form of exhibitionism which attracted the wrath of Harold Rosenberg:

The more exactly he grasps, whether by instinct or
through study, the existing element of sameness in
people, the more successful is the mass culture-maker.
Indeed, so committed is he to the idea that all men are
alike that he may even fancy that there exists a kind of
human dead centre in which everyone is identical to
everyone else, and that if he can hit that psychic bull's
eye then he can make all mankind twitch at once.

The art world of the last century, which was rejecting traditional forms of art, felt equal antipathy towards mass culture.
This saw artists of all kinds, not just painters but musicians and
writers, push the boundaries of the arts in a movement that
became dubbed as the 'avant-garde', the advanced guard. The
military comparison was exact, as the avant-garde had a mission to revolutionise the way people saw art. It also reinforced,
perhaps unwittingly, the image of 'Cultureberg' as a collective
of creative people living outside the mores of traditional society. The term 'avant-garde' was first used in the early 1960s,
and literally ushered in the 'Summer of Love' and the cultural
and social revolution that ensued.

One of the artists who defined the sixties, and laid the
template for the art of the late twentieth and early twenty-first
centuries, was Andy Warhol. He became famous initially for his
'pop art', painting everyday objects like a Campbell's soup can
and a Coca-Cola bottle, and later producing iconic images of
Marilyn Monroe and Elvis. He was openly gay at a time when it
was still illegal and classed as a mental illness. At his studio in
New York, the Factory, he gathered together a unique collection of people, ranging from intellectuals to drag queens,
bohemians, celebrities, vagrants and wealthy patrons; a weird,
louche world that achieved artistic fame in its own right. He
made underground films starring unknown actors, and sponsored the archetypal cult band of all time, the Velvet Underground. On all levels – artistic, social, sexual – he operated
almost entirely outside of mainstream culture, society, and the

law. Despite, or perhaps because of, this he rapidly became wealthy and famous, and his works were 'the bellwether of the art world', according to one critic. Needless to say he was vilified for turning art into a business. He also took art in a completely unexpected direction with his 'oxidation' paintings – canvases prepared with copper paint that was then oxidised by urinating on them. Perhaps the ability to sell body fluids as art is the ultimate form of exhibitionism.

Warhol was to become, after his death, one of the most sought after artists for the collectors. Prices for art began to skyrocket, and not just for new work. In 1987, the Australian businessman Alan Bond paid $54 million for van Gogh's 'Irises', at the time a world record for a single painting. The auction captured the public imagination, making the national news, and triggering a price stampede for collectable work. High-end art joined the mansion, the yacht and the private jet as an entry card to the club of the super-rich. Alan Bond borrowed money he had no hope of repaying to secure 'Irises', some of which was loaned by Sotheby's, the auctioneers. In a twist to the tale, it was said by some that this deal was done to inflate the price of works of art. Whatever the reason, the current record for a painting is $250 million, for Cézanne's 'Card Players', owned by the Royal Family of Qatar. Only the seriously wealthy can now play this game.

This has not been lost on the artists themselves. Although a favourite image of the artist is one of the lonely genius starving in a garret – van Gogh painted 'Irises' in an asylum – there are many who have become rich in their own lifetime. Picasso was one, Warhol another. The modern era has truly witnessed the emergence of the artist who is not only a creative genius, but also an expert in self-promotion. The American installation artist Jeff Koons began by selling subscriptions to the Museum of Modern Art in New York – he was their most successful salesman – and had a career as a commodities broker before becoming a conceptual artist. He uses the language of the market to describe his work, openly seeking to 'increase my market share'. 'The great artists will be the great negotiators,' is another of his aphorisms, which has become a mantra for the new wave of conceptual artists. The best known is Damien Hirst, a conceptual artist who achieved fame as one of the Young British Artists, or YBAs, who flourished in the 1990s London art scene. Their work was bought by the collector Charles Saatchi, who also sponsored Hirst's early career. Saatchi made his fortune in an advertising agency, Saatchi and Saatchi, who were responsible for the 'Labour isn't working' ad which helped propel Margaret Thatcher to power. The YBAs were noted for their shock tactics, and gained a reputation for wild living and excess. Although firmly rooted in the artistic tradition of opposition to conventional society, they were noted for their entrepreneurial spirit.

Hirst now operates in much the same way as the old masters, employing assistants to perform much of the actual work on his paintings and sculptures. He is a multimillionaire, and that fact in itself sums up the strange world of modern art. Here we have this edgy artist, producing ground-breaking art, who almost certainly is viewed as an outsider by ordinary society. And yet he has arrived there courtesy of a man who made his fortune in advertising, traditionally anathema to the avant-garde, and one, moreover, who helped the party of the Establishment, the Conservatives, get elected. And he is rich and famous and powerful, ticking all the conventional boxes for success in a capitalist society. For anyone brought up in the sixties, like me, who thought of society in terms of 'straight' and 'alternative', the absorption of artists like Hirst into the mainstream is unsettling. Rich, secular, Western society is capable of assimilating virtually anything, it seems.

The twentieth century saw the surreal, bizarre and the outré become accepted as the new high art. What happened, then, to artists who were still painting in a traditional style? The answer is, they continued to exhibit, but they had restricted access to the temples of culture. Modern art was more fashionable, but even that became sidelined in an attempt to broaden the cultural horizon beyond 'dead, white, European males'. In the United States in particular, museums began to give equal prominence to artists from other cultures, provoking violent debate about the quality of work on offer. The writer Lynne Munson, in her book *Exhibitionism,* detailed how the art world of the late twentieth century was taken over by progressives determined to shift the cultural balance, valuing fashionability over technical skill, reorganising museums and devaluing the traditional study of art. The effect was to control what type of art would be funded and exhibited, which in turn would affect what the public could see. The takeover of an institution by a small number of highly motivated people determined to make it conform to their world view is not confined to art alone, of course, but is symptomatic of late twentieth century Western society. It is exhibitionism used as a demonstration of power and conformity. You will think what I think and see what I see.

But the old art would not go away. The 2000s saw the rise of the blockbuster exhibition, when museums and galleries would mount a show by a single artist, using their collection and borrowing from other museums. The most popular, by far, are shows dedicated to the 'classics': Leonardo, the French Impressionists, Turner and Picasso. To curate such a show successfully brings fame both to the curator and the museum, as well as large amounts of money. Even though art as we know it has gone off in some unexpected directions, the desire to view art has never been greater. Some shows got so many visitors that the 'viewing experience' was severely restricted, causing some galleries to restrict numbers. The National Gallery decided to do this with a recent Leonardo exhibition, with the result that it sold out almost immediately. Exhibitionism is big business.

It can also be a fairly murky one. The Barnes Foundation in Philadelphia contains the collection of Albert C. Barnes, a chemist who made his fortune with a drug used to treat gonorrhoea. He invested this fortune in art, which given the rackety nature of some artists is somewhat appropriate. He began collecting in the 1920s and amassed a collection of 181 paintings, which included works by Cézanne, Matisse, van Gogh, Rubens, Titian, Manet and many others. Virtually all the great nineteenth and early twentieth century painters were represented and the collection is estimated to be worth $25 *billion* dollars. Barnes built a special home for the collection, arranged the works personally and endowed it primarily as a school where young artists could study the pictures. It was open to the public on two days a week only, which was difficult enough as it was located in a residential area of Montgomery County, with a limited transport infrastructure. Barnes died unmarried with no offspring, and left strict instructions in his will that the pictures remain *in situ*, as a place for students to study, with public access strictly controlled.

Problems arose when the fabric of the building began to deteriorate. The Foundation was apparently running out of money, and it was argued they needed to expand the number of trustees and try and source funds from elsewhere. In the 1990s the director of the Barnes Foundation made the controversial decision to send selected works on a world tour. As this went against the express wishes of Albert Barnes, the Friends of the Barnes Foundation mounted a legal challenge. They lost. The Foundation continued to have documented financial problems and was being circled by other bodies desperate to have control over the collection. Three non-profit making charities agreed to help, but with one condition – that the foundation relocate to a more central site. A furious legal battle ensued, which eventually decided in favour of moving the collection. This finally happened in May 2012. A documentary about the legal and political machinations involved in the decision, *The Art of the Steal*, was made in 2009, coming down heavily in favour of the Friends of the Barnes Foundation, who opposed the move. Critics claimed it was one-sided, but the message was obvious. As the critic Roger Ebert, of the *Chicago Sun-Times* wrote:

It was perfectly clear what Barnes specified in his will. It was drawn up by the best legal minds. It is clear that what happened to his collection was against his wishes. It is clear that the city fathers acted in obviation of those wishes, and were upheld in a court of appeal. What is finally clear: It doesn't matter a damn what your will says if you have $25 billion and the politicians and the establishment want it.

So, the right to leave instructions as to how and where your pictures are exhibited means nothing if someone else wants control of the exhibition badly enough. The desire to be the exhibitor is as strong as any creative urge. I am sure the general public can understand the creative desire of the artist, but I don't think any of us truly understand the mindset of people who are desperate to be in the public eye, like politicians and the people who wanted to get their hands on the Barnes Collection.

And lo, we reach the conclusion. I hope to have shown how exhibitionism is not merely confined to the artist and the work of art, but to the collectors, auctioneers, curators, charitable foundations and all the other characters in the vast back country of the art world. And that also a work of art may not be what it appears at face value, that the purpose of its exhibition may not be straightforward. Finally, I hope that you will be able to understand why a dead fish in formaldehyde is a zoology exhibit, while a shark in a tank with the title 'The Physical Impossibility of Death in the Mind of Someone Living' is worth $12 million dollars. Grasp that and you've got art and exhibitionism nailed down.

5

Exhibitionism as public display 2: the performing arts

The ability to stand up and perform in front of people almost certainly goes back to the first human society, but it was our old friends the Greeks who gave us the theatre we recognise today. Early Greek theatre did not feature individual actors, but choruses who moved the story on collectively. According to popular legend it was the poet Thespis who first introduced the concept of an individual actor giving a performance, creating different characters by the use of masks and costumes. In doing so he 'invented' acting, and a new genre of plays known as tragedies, as opposed to the existing comedies. Being the sole actor in a performance meant that Thespis could take his show on the road, which he did, creating the touring company. (If there are any actors reading this, I expect they're muttering, 'Thank you, Thespis,' through clenched teeth.) It is interesting that the purpose behind the earliest form of public performance was to make people laugh or cry, to work on the emotions. As we shall see, the emotions are the key to exhibitionism as public display.

Thespis lives on in the term 'thespian', a generic term for actors, often used ironically. It can also describe a character trait in the lay public, as in, 'fancies himself as a bit of a thespian'. It has been used to describe the status of an actor, usually being associated with the stage, and implying that the actor had played the grand roles – the Lears, the Hamlets, and so on. A proper thespian is one of the greats, far above a mere journeyman actor. Again, within the profession it could describe the performer who has an exaggerated grasp of the mannerisms of acting, an 'old thesp', also described as an 'ac-tor'. The term 'ham' actor, or 'old ham' is also used to describe the more obviously theatrical performers, actors who can only play a caricature of themselves. But they are in a minority. The profession itself displays a wide range of acting styles, ranging from the minimalist actor, through the competent but unspectacular jobbing actor, the ham actor, and reaching a pinnacle in the greats, actors who bring real power and conviction to their roles.

So where does exhibitionism fit into the acting profession? Do we draw a line somewhere, separating 'normal' actors from 'exhibitionist' actors? Surely there are two completely different psyches at play, the actor who is interested in playing the part as well as they can versus the actor who makes the part a vehicle for self-promotion?

Laurence Olivier, later Lord Olivier, and possibly the greatest actor of the twentieth century, had no doubt where the motivation lay. 'Acting,' he said, 'is a masochistic form of exhibitionism. It is not quite the occupation for an adult.' This is an interesting observation from someone who had mastered the disciplines of both stagecraft and film work. Olivier is saying that all actors are, at heart, exhibitionists, yet with some it is a compulsion rather than a pleasure. He also hints that performers are mired somewhere between childhood and adulthood in their personal development. If this implies a fairly complex mix of character traits, then the personalities of actors themselves would bear this out. Some are extremely sensitive to any imagined slight, and like to exert absolute control over their image, while others are self-deprecating to an extreme. Marlon Brando, a notoriously 'difficult' actor, once said: 'An actor is someone who, if you ain't talking about him, ain't listening'. He also remarked, 'The principle benefit acting has afforded me is the money to pay for my psychoanalysis'.

Laurence Olivier was the finest stage actor of his generation, and Brando arguably the best film actor. The two disciplines contain similarities, yet are obviously different in that on the stage the actor is directly exhibiting to an audience, while the film actor is performing for an audience yet unseen. And it gets more complicated, because the broadcast media has thrown up yet another branch of public display – the hordes of presenters, newsreaders, disc jockeys, weathermen and all those people who are not quite actors but who nonetheless are performing. We now have this vast network of people who impinge directly on our everyday lives, and who sometimes are little more than 'famous for being famous'.

Ah yes, you might say, but the presenters and so on aren't like actors, they're just doing a job, they're not selling themselves. To which I would reply – pull the other one. If you think that is being unduly cynical, then try the following exercise. Name five TV or radio presenters, with their occupations: newsreader, radio presenter, and so on. Now name five cabinet ministers, with their departments. Struggling? OK, name another five presenters. Now another five cabinet ministers. I bet you can get ten presenters, easily, but I expect most of you failed to get ten ministers. The fact that their names are in the public domain is exhibitionism of a sort, and you can bet that most cabinet ministers wouldn't mind the public profile of the average media pundit. There is also a hypnotic quality to the fame of TV presenters because their names get repeated so often that they become lodged in the memory. Why do I know, for example, that the BBC's media correspondent is called Torin Douglas? Or the occupations of John Pienarr or Nick Robinson? Because on a daily basis we hear, 'Over to our political correspondent, Nick Robinson … ' and, 'Nick Robinson for the BBC, Westminster'. It is a kind of mantra, the sort of hook beloved by advertising executives attempting to create a brand.

So how did it come to this? How did a craft, which, up until fifty years ago, still largely existed in its own world, become the teeming, multifaceted, invasive supranational monster it is today? There are lots of reasons, and to identify them we have to start at the origins of modern entertainment, when actors became famous for their skill alone.

The history of the performing arts mirrors that of representational art. The crafts first flourished in Ancient Greece, with the emergence of Thespis and the creation of comedies and tragedies. The first plays were linked with the festival of Dionysius, the Greek god of wine and fertility. Ancient Greece also gave us an architectural legacy, some of the most impressive ruins being the theatres the Greeks used to stage the plays. The theatre at Delphi had 35 rows and could seat 5000 people, indicating the importance of performance art to the concept of civilisation. The names of over 100 playwrights are known, and complete texts by Aristophanes, Sophocles, Aeschylus and others have survived to the present day and are still being performed. The Romans continued the theatrical tradition, remaining true to the Greek templates of comedies and tragedies, with Terence, Plautus and Seneca being notable Roman playwrights. The Romans also added a new dimension to the art of public display with their gladiatorial contests and battle re-enactments inside the Coliseum, and although these were 'entertainments' they were not strictly art.

Following the collapse of the Roman Empire, drama, like art, disappeared, until it resurfaced to serve a religious purpose. Enactments of religious themes were performed in the Dark Ages, some of which were written by Hrosvitha, a German canoness. These are the first recorded plays by a female playwright, as well as being among the few surviving works from that period.

In the later Middle Ages the religious themes coalesced into the more recognisable form of the mystery play, where biblical themes were enacted out, often in a 'theatre of the round', where the action moved from stage to stage round the circumference of the circle. The plays were often local to a town or village, and the 'actors' came from the indigenous population. My native Cornwall was an especially fertile ground for these performances. Some of the plays have survived, the best known being the Ordinalia trilogy, which tells the story of the origin of the world, the Passion of Christ, and the resurrection of the Lord. The primitive theatres, known as Plen-an-Gwarry's, or playing places, have also survived, simple circular outdoor arenas enclosed by grassy banks.

Professional actors began to appear in the late Middle Ages. Both Richard III and Henry VII retained companies of actors and many of the great houses had specially built galleries for performances. The subject matter of the performances was becoming more varied. Playwrights in France and Germany began producing farces, a new type of light drama which included depictions of sex and bodily functions. Performance in England was important enough for Henry VIII to establish an 'Office of Revels' in 1545.

The really important period for dramatic art in England was the Elizabethan age, which saw the creation of purpose built theatres and the emergence of our greatest playwright, William Shakespeare. Religious subjects in drama, as in art, were banned by the new Protestant faith, so the new playwrights turned back to comedies and tragedies as templates, and added a new genre in the form of the history plays. The actors came from the old companies attached to wealthy households, becoming licensed touring players. These replaced the local casts of mystery plays. By the early seventeenth century there were a dozen purpose-built theatres in London, and more were to open in the provinces.

Although drama was popular in Elizabethan times, the status of actors was questionable, occupying a position outside of polite society. Christopher Marlowe, actor and playwright, was killed in a tavern brawl and Ben Johnson killed another actor in a duel. Acting and writing were not particularly well rewarded, and, like art, were often dependant on patronage. There is no evidence that actors were regarded as anything other than simple craftsmen.

Theatre flourished in the time of Charles I, but was then banned in the Commonwealth. It was restored under Charles II, and saw the creation of a new type of comedy, Restoration comedy, which reflected the raffish life of London and was often sexually explicit. This led to the appearance of the first actresses, of which Nell Gwynn, the mistress of Charles II, was one of the first. The status of actors also changed, performing skill being recognised as an art in itself. The first celebrity actor was Thomas Betterton, who was somewhat stout, with small eyes and a 'low voice' yet who had considerable dramatic power. Samuel Pepys thought his Hamlet was so good it was, 'beyond imagination'. Charles II licensed two companies to produce plays: the Kings Company and the Dukes Company, both of whom now competed for the best actors and actresses. This in turn led to an improvement in the financial circumstances of the acting profession, although one suspects that it quickly evolved into the pyramid it is today, with the wealthy few at the summit and the rest on the breadline.

The Restoration also saw the creation of the 'Restoration spectacular', a show which featured music, dance, elaborate costumes and special effects (trapdoors and the like). This became the template for the modern 'spectacular', where the show itself, rather than the individual performers, was the exhibition.

The actors of the early eighteenth century favoured a rather bombastic style of acting which was probably necessary because of the poor lighting and acoustics of the early theatres. As these were improved, a greater range of technique could be employed, which saw the emergence of one of the great names in British theatrical history, David Garrick. He rose to prominence as an actor, manager and playwright, and changed both the craft of acting and the quality of the performance. Garrick brought a naturalistic style to acting which was the antithesis of the loud, declamatory style, causing the actor James Quin to

remark, 'if this young fellow be right, then we are all wrong'.
One critic told Garrick that, 'he never knew what acting was
until [he] appeared'. But it was not to everyone's taste. The
critic Theophilius Cibber listed his faults:

> His over-fondance of extravagant attitudes, frequently
> affected starts, convulsive twitching's, jerking's of the
> body, sprawling of the fingers, flapping the breasts and
> pockets; a set of mechanical motions in constant use;
> the caricatures of gestures, suggested by a pert vivacity;
> his pantomimical manner of acting every word in a
> sentence, his unnatural pauses, his forced conceits; his
> wilful neglect of harmony, even where the round period
> of well-expressed noble sentiment demands a graceful
> cadence in the delivery.

I have quoted this at length because it explains the unique
position actors find themselves in, and why they can become
quite sensitive to criticism. If you read the above critique again,
what does it tell you? Does Cibber have anything positive to
say about Garrick? No, he does not. He actually criticises every
single component of Garrick's acting technique, and although
he stops short of saying that Garrick is a complete failure as a
human being, he has denigrated everything else. It is a savage
and personal review.

And this is the difference with the performing arts. Criticism
of painters and musicians did not really get into its stride until
the nineteenth century, yet here, in 1756, we have a critic
ripping into an actor. It is less than 100 years after the Restoration, yet the theatre critic is already established, willing to
praise or savage any production. A painter can retreat to his
studio after a critical disaster, but an actor has to go back out,
night after night, often in the certain knowledge that he is
going to get a rough ride. To be an actor is to be an exhibitionist, but all too often that exhibition is not to everyone's taste. It
must require a quite extraordinary psychological make-up to

tolerate this life, and it explains why so many actors retreat into a reclusive private life. David Garrick is revered in the profession not just for his skill but because he attempted, in his role as a theatre manager, to modify the behaviour of the audience.

By the nineteenth century, the entertainment industry was gaining the breadth that we recognise today. The early part of the century saw Shakespeare revived. Melodramas – popular works whose exaggerated plots and strong characterisation appealed to the emotions, were imported from France. In the middle of the century, the music hall brought the various forms of rural, fairground and public house entertainments under a single roof. The type of show found in the music hall was eminently suited to the exhibitionist performer, being loud, brassy, rude, and often very funny. The performance itself was a mixture of popular songs, comedy, specialist acts (jugglers, acrobats), ventriloquists, female impersonators, puppet shows, and anything else which would entertain the mainly working class audience. The origins of much of our modern entertainment lie back in those Victorian music halls, and they were still going in the 1950s, until television killed them off.

The appeal of music hall rested on the character of the performer. One of the best known was Marie Lloyd, a singer and comedienne who could turn the most innocent of lyrics into a bawdy ballad by the use of suggestive pauses, winks, and innuendo. 'I sits among the cabbages and peas,' a seemly harmless song about the joys of gardening, became a story about outdoor urination. Another song, 'Oh! Mr Porter' goes like this:

> Oh! Mr Porter, what shall I do?
> I wanted to go to Birmingham and they've taken me on to Crewe.
> Take me back to London, as quickly as you can,
> Oh! Mr Porter, what a silly girl I am.

In Marie Lloyd's hands, this simple lyric turns into a story about a girl 'going too far', when petting has got out of hand and she ends up having sex. If this seems tame by modern standards, then you have to remember that Victorian morality was much stricter than ours. Marie Lloyd was hauled before several committees to answer charges of lewdness, although she was never prosecuted. She walked a very fine line with consummate skill, and it was her performance, what she did with the material, which made her a star. She also led the prototype celebrity life, marrying three times and turning to drink. When she died, three days after a drunken performance, 100,000 people lined the streets at her funeral.

There was now a gap opening up between popular entertainment and highbrow theatre. The most celebrated actors of the upmarket Victorian theatre were Henry Irvine, the first actor to be knighted, and the actress Helen Terry. At the Lyceum theatre they produced critically acclaimed productions of Shakespeare and other playwrights. Irvine played Shylock in *The Merchant of Venice* with sympathy, making him a different character from the curmudgeonly Jewish merchant of popular opinion. It is thought that Irvine and Terry were lovers, one of the original 'celebrity couples'. We are seeing the emergence of the romance and edgy sexuality which surrounds the acting profession.

Around the turn of the century, the gap between music hall and highbrow theatre was filled with a wide range of entertainment, from the comic operas of Gilbert and Sullivan through to plays by Shaw and Wilde. Edwardian musical comedies were popular and saw the invention of the chorus line, a troupe of young women singing or performing synchronised dance moves, often in extravagant costumes. In a strange twist to the story of exhibitionism, these girls often became the target for 'stage door johnnies', English gentlemen who haunted the stage door hoping to date, or even marry, one of them. The Gaiety Girls were one such troupe, described as, 'polite, well-spoken young women'. Elsewhere, showgirls in less salubrious shows were regarded as closer to prostitutes, and the United States 'burlesque' (our vaudeville, although coarser) eventually evolved into striptease. The stripper illustrated the complex nature of public display, on the face of it being simply titillating, but containing undercurrents of power, control, and even art. Although it had its seedy origins, nudity became absorbed into mainstream culture through the twentieth century.

The biggest change in performance as public display also occurred in the twentieth century with the invention of cinema. Up until then, actors and performers in the theatres and music halls were, even if famous, connected directly with the audience. People could see them physically, and form impressions not just from their performance but from the hordes of subliminal impressions you make when you see someone in the flesh. Although they are in a different place from you, they are 'real'. And the live audience is also part of the performance, however unwittingly. Some entertainers, most obviously comedians but also stage actors, have this ability to feed off their audience to reach new heights of performance. One of the magical qualities of live theatre are those occasions when the actors and audience are in harmony, somehow making the performance bigger than the component parts. As the actress Shelley Winters put it:

> Every now and then, when you're onstage, you hear the best sound a player can hear. It is the sound you can't get in movies or on television. It is the sound of a wonderful, deep silence that means you've hit them where they live.

The qualities required by a film actor are very different. They are at one remove from their audience, creating art in the confines of the studio, often putting together performances out of sequence that only become a 'whole' when the sequences are spliced together in the editing room. The techniques required are very different, relying on often subtle facial expression (hard to read in the theatre), absolute control over movement and a completely different vocal range. The lack of an audience means that film actors can cultivate a mystique quite different from a stage actor. In extreme cases they can become almost mythical figures. The first screen heartthrob was Rudolph Valentino, whose death at the age of 31 prompted hysteria among his female fans. Over 100 police were required to control fans outside the funeral parlour, and it is rumoured that some fans were so distraught they resorted to suicide. In an early warning of the strange world of movie fame, four black-shirted bodyguards appeared, allegedly sent by the Italian leader Benito Mussolini. This was later revealed to be a publicity stunt.

In another earlier premonition of the perils of movie fame, a Chicago newspaper thought that Valentino's well-groomed appearance was leading to the feminisation of American men. The article was prompted by the appearance of pink talcum powder in a hotel vending machine. Valentino sought the advice of writer H. L. Menken, who described the actor thus:

> It was not that trifling Chicago incident that was bothering him: it was the whole gross futility of his life. Had he achieved out of nothing a vast and dizzy success? Then that success was hollow as well as vast – a colossal and preposterous nothing. Was he acclaimed by yelling multitudes? Then every time they yelled he found himself blushing inside. The thing, at the start, must have only bewildered him, but in those last days, unless I am a worse psychologist than even those professors of psychology, it was revolting him. Worse, it was making him afraid. Here was a young man who was living daily the dream of millions of men. Here was one who was catnip to women. Here was one who had wealth and fame. And here was one who was very unhappy.

So the peculiar sense of being and nothingness which some actors describe, and the strangely depressing nature of fame itself, was not something which developed as the movie business became big business, but was present right from the start of the motion picture industry. The description of Rudolph Valentino by H. L. Menken seems to vindicate Olivier's description of acting as a masochistic form of exhibitionism. Certainly public acclaim, or fame, the ultimate aim of most performers, would seem to be a particularly poisoned chalice.

So who would want to do this? Does the urge for fame overwhelm the more rational side of the actor's personality? Is it something which he or she cannot resist, a calling? Or is the motivation the desire to create a work of artistic merit, with fame as an unfortunate side effect? The number of famous actors who complain about the intrusions into their private life would seem to bear this out, but as an enthusiastic reader of the utterly cynical British press I have my doubts about that. And finally, could anyone be an actor, or is it a profession characterised by a particular set of personality traits?

The answer is that anyone *can* be an actor, as long as he or she is determined enough. It does help, however, to have a certain set of personality characteristics, and to find out what they are we have to go back to Carl Gustav Jung and the origins of modern psychology. Jung noticed during his consultations that patients were not a random, sporadic mass of personalities, but fell into quite distinct groups. He began to identify the ways people presented information, made decisions and organised their lives. He particularly defined Extroversion as people who get their energy by reacting with the external world, and Introversion as those who need solitude and peace to recharge their batteries. His work was taken up by two American women, Katherine Myers and her daughter Isabel Myers Briggs, and together they created the Myers Brigg Type Index, a personality test to identify the different types.

The Index split personalities between four different parameters. The first, where one gets one's energy: Extraversion, E, or Introversion, I, which we have already encountered. The second, how we take in information, is split between Sensing, S, where the person prefers concrete information and facts and figures, and Intuition, N, where the person prefers concepts and abstract thinking. The next pair describe how we make decisions, the Thinker, T, using logic and cause and effect reasoning, while the person with a preference for Feeling, F, will make decisions based on personal factors, how the decision will impact on people. Finally there is the way we react to the world, the person with a preference for Judging, J, liking closure and routines, and the Perceiver, P, preferring to keep things open ended, often until the last minute (or beyond). The result is a four letter type, for example ENTJ. There are sixteen possible 'types'.

The psychologist David Kiersey grouped these into four temperaments, the Idealist, Rationalist, Guardian, and Artisan. Each contained four of the personality types, and these were divided into two subgroups. The Artisan subgroup was divided into the 'Operator' group, whose two members were the ESTP Promoter, and the ISTP, Crafter, and the 'Entertainer' group whose members were the ISFP, Composer, and the ESFP, Performer. Although these tests cannot be definitive, there appears to be a psychological basis for some people's need to perform.

If we analyse the components of Keirsey's temperaments for the Performer we see that the logic holds. People with a preference for Extraversion gain their energy from reacting with other people, the Sensing preference means they are centred on the moment, the Feeling preference reflects their interest in people, and their preference for Perceiving means they are flexible and spontaneous. The Performer is likely to be surrounded by people, be engaging conversationalists, enjoy the good things in life, and, more importantly, like others to be enjoying themselves. They get a buzz from being in the limelight, and are good at improvising and coping with unexpected interruptions. They do not cope well with anxiety and generally do not seek scholastic or theoretical pursuits. Not all ESFP's are actors, of course, but analysis of the personality types of performers shows an above average concentration of that personality type in the profession. Outside of acting they will be salesmen, teachers, and nurses, and you will have met them as the 'life and soul of the party' or even the bloke who is a great joke teller in the pub. They tend to be remembered.

Many people with a preference for Extroversion can be, in a sense, exhibitionists, in that they will enjoy being the centre of attention. If you look at the terms used to describe the personality types with this preference, you find words like 'leader', 'motivator', and 'commander', as well as 'performer'. They can be the 'stand out' people in society.

The danger with all these forms of personality tests is that people see them to be definitive. They are guides, no more, just lamps in the fog. The trouble is that once you have a 'type', you tend to think of what you can, or more importantly, cannot do. Just because certain types are drawn to certain jobs does not mean that other types cannot do that job. Any type can do any job. There is also no sense of value in a personality type. An ESFP may be an absolutely lousy 'performer', their preferences being just that, preferences. And we also have to remember that overlaying all this is the world in which we live, which colours everything. And this is why, I think, the performing arts are filled with such a mix of characters, because of all the forms of exhibitionism, the performing arts carry the possibility of fame. It doesn't matter what personality type you are, in a world dominated by the broadcast media, you are going to think that the performing arts could be your ticket out of obscurity.

To return to acting as public display, it is important to emphasise the care that goes into producing a professional work, in both the script and production, and in the training of individual actors. At the turn of the last century the nature of performance began to be examined, most notably by the Russian actor and director Constantin Stanislavski. He observed that actors did not necessarily give the same performance every time, yet their best performances all contained the same characteristics. He believed that you could break down these performances and analyse the various movements, gestures, and vocal techniques which made the performance special. And, more importantly, that it could be taught. Actors were encouraged to study the text minutely, not just to learn their lines but to gain a psychological insight into the characters. This would help them to 'become' the character, to play them for real. He also studied the relationship between emotion and movement, exploring in particular the sequence of events in that relationship. For example, if you suddenly see a venomous snake ahead on the path in front of you, do you feel afraid first and then run away, or do you run first and then feel afraid? To most of us the answer is immaterial, as long as you get away, but to the artist trying to deliver a credible performance it is a key question.

The relationship between emotion and acting, especially movement, took the techniques of acting into a new dimension. If a part requires an actor to cry, it is more believable if he or she holds their hands up to their eyes and bows their head. Similarly it is easier to believe that a character has suffered crushing disappointment if their features are downcast and their shoulders slumped.

Stanislavski also encouraged actors to use experiences from their own life to help them play similar scenes by a character. The creation of believable theatre began to draw on psychological factors as well as the straightforward interpretation of the text. Stanford Meisner, one of the members of the revolutionary Group Theatre in the USA, took this a stage further. He thought that using one's own experiences to help create a character meant that the character was still not 'real'. He used interpersonal techniques to help free the actors from 'self' and create a completely authentic character. It is important to stress this concept, because although actors talk about it, few of us realise the preparation that goes into performing such a role. The whole aim of modern performance is to deliver an authentic version of the play or script, with characters that are 'real', not just aspects of a particular actor. If it works, and it requires a lot of practice, the actor can create a work of art. The founder of Group Theatre was Lee Strasberg, and it was from the work of this group that the concept of method acting became famous. Some of his pupils are among the most famous of Hollywood actors including Paul Newman, Dustin Hoffman, Al Pacino, Anne Bancroft and Marilyn Monroe.

The effect of all this work is quite complex. To be an actor is to be on public display, to be an exhibitionist. Yet since the twentieth century, and up to the present day, to be an actor it is necessary to strip away your own ego and replace it with the ego, as best as you can manage it, of your character. The better you are at doing that, the more successful you become, and taken to its ultimate conclusion you can become anyone. This is a schizophrenic form of exhibitionism, being famous for your ability to become someone else. And performing must take a huge psychological toll on the actor, let alone the downside, for some, of being a celebrity. If you really live the part then it must be exhausting, and I have a great deal of admiration for the performers who are willing to do this. As we will see later, it can come at a price.

While method acting was developing in America, the English stage remained (fairly) rooted in the classical tradition of acting, concentrating on the quality of the external performance. I think it is fair to say that some of our grander actors rather looked down on the new American system. In the film *Marathon Man*, Dustin Hoffman appeared on set looking tired and dishevelled, having not slept for two days. When his co-star, Laurence Olivier, asked him what was up, he explained that he was getting into character. To which Olivier apparently replied, 'Try acting, dear boy. Much healthier'. (This anecdote is repeatedly denied, but I have put it in because you should never let the truth get in the way of a good story.)

Of all the types of exhibitionism, acting would seem to be the most straightforward. Yet, as I hope to have demonstrated, it is not quite what it appears. At one end of the spectrum there is the actor who acquires conventional skills to play the classic parts, at the other there is the actor who is able to cast aside their own personality to invest wholly in their new character. Ultimately they may be the same thing. But in both they are seeking to put themselves somehow in the background. They don't wish fame for themselves, they want to be recognised for their ability.

Although, is that altogether true? Do we watch a show or film because it has a certain actor in it, or do we go because we want to see that particular performance? For example, one of the most universally acclaimed stage performances in recent years was Mark Rylance in *Jerusalem*. Would I want to see the play again with another lead? No. Would I like to see Mark Rylance in something else? Yes. Would I like to see Mark Rylance in *Romeo and Juliet*? No, because I can't stand the play. Go figure, as the Americans say.

And there is the other side of the coin, the position of the actor. Someone like Clint Eastwood gets such a strong 'brand' that it is difficult for him to escape his on-screen persona, although to his credit he has produced a varied and high quality body of work. But for most of us, he is the alpha male of *The Outlaw Josey Wales* or *Dirty Harry*, the uncompromising outsider, the unforgiving hard man who explains to the wounded bank robber after a shootout:

> I know what you're thinking. You're thinking, has he fired five shots or six? And to tell you the truth, in all this excitement, I've clean forgot myself. But seeing as this is a .44 Magnum, the most powerful handgun in the world, and could blow your head clean off, you got to ask yourself one question. Do I feel lucky? Well, do ya, punk?

How we beta males (all right, beta plus) wish we were that tough. But what does it say about Clint himself, I wonder? He has played that kind of character so often that perhaps he is saying that this is him, that at least a part of him is the genuine tough guy. At the end of the above speech he gives a kind of weird smile, which hints at a more complex inner life than that displayed by Dirty Harry himself. Perhaps this is also a sign of the complexity of fame that we see these actors so often that we feel that we 'know' them, or at least, can speculate on their natures from the clues they give us in their performances.

Fame is the two-faced reward for exhibitionism in the performing arts, especially the cinema. Actors who don't wish to be famous describe it as a monster, which I believe that it is. I can see how someone who is focused on their craft finds it irksome to be mobbed, and who get roundly criticised when they allow their real personalities, which may be the total opposite to their 'brand', to emerge. Some are dismissive of this duality, like the actor Kevin Bacon, who stated in a recent interview: 'Show me an actor who doesn't want to be famous and I'll show you a liar'. Whatever the motivation, they develop protective mechanisms – the entourage, the vetting, and the carefully managed interviews. At its most absurd, the public clamour for an entirely artificial construct, the 'star', who obliges by creating that construct as a self-defence mechanism. This is exhibitionism as what? A world of smoke and mirrors inviting the worship of a personality that doesn't exist? Maybe, but there is a whole world out there devoted to keeping the show on the road.

So far we have concentrated on the traditional relationship between the production and the audience, in that a film or show is presented to an audience who are relatively passive consumers of the product. In the previous chapter about art, we saw the emergence of new ways of looking at art in the twentieth century, and a similar thing happened with theatre and film. Experimental theatre, especially, broke down the barriers between audience and performer, and between performers. The audience were included in the production, often physically, and sometimes left to use their imagination to complete the experience. One of the pioneers of this approach was Samuel Beckett, whose two act play, *Waiting for Godot*, was described as a play where nothing happens – twice. It is a stripped down text that leaves the audience to fill in the gaps with private speculation. The two main characters, Vladimir and Estragon, are waiting for Godot, although who that might be, no one knows. In the meantime they engage in discussions, fall asleep, swap hats, and wait. A rich man, Pozzo, passes through with a slave. They share a meal. Pozzo and the slave leave. Vladamir and Estragon cannot remember if they are in the right place at the right time. Or if Godot is coming, or what he is going to do if he gets there. Godot never arrives, but the play continues on its elliptical and allusive way. It is a work which gets its power through the imagination of the audience.

The term 'Theatre of the Absurd' was coined to describe this new type of drama which portrayed the human condition as purposeless and meaningless, with communication becoming random and illogical. Later playwrights would include Harold Pinter, who notably employed silence as a dramatic tool. This type of work is powerful because the jagged shards of dialogue hint at something, while at the same time digging at emotions you may not want to experience in the theatre, like bewilderment, disgust, fear, irritation and hatred. In terms of exhibitionism, they are difficult to classify, because they exist outside of the traditional purpose of entertainment, both for the product and the performer. You don't come out of a Pinter play feeling the same as after a James Bond movie. You have not been entertained, you have been challenged. And whereas you may envy Daniel Craig, or at least think of him as a star, Pinter's characters are odd, somewhat creepy people you may not want to meet backstage. It is, in effect, a return to pure drama, where the actors are mere vessels for conveying truth of the play, where there is no sense of their off stage personalities at all. And this is not just confined to difficult or challenging work. Under the blockbuster films, and star-led productions of classic drama, there are a whole host of companies producing a variety of work, which, because the cast is not famous, help the audience to focus on the production.

We have discussed the hinterland around performance, and the challenges involved in trying to subsume the ego in the act of artistic exhibitionism. There are occasions, however, when the ego – or more importantly, the mannerisms – of the actor are the selling point for a film or play. Someone like Bill Nighy has combined a set of unique mannerisms, both vocal and physical, which make him extremely watchable. Of course he plays a variety of roles, but his presence in a film or TV programme will make it a draw. The trouble is, once an actor like that has achieved fame, it is difficult for them to return to different parts.

There are actors, however, who make a career by playing the same character over and over again. They may go by different names, and they are usually in comedy or light entertainment. Very often the character is over-the-top, a caricature almost. One thinks of Windsor Davies in the series *It Ain't Half Hot, Mum,* a parody of the apoplectic sergeant major who dominated his scenes. John Inman became a household name as the camp shop assistant Mr Humphries in the sitcom *Are You Being Served?* and took the personality onto the pantomime stage. The actor Derek Nimmo played slightly dim members of the upper classes, and very English clergymen. All these roles are classic exhibitionism, because they are ordinary occupations given an extravagant flourish. If you think of more modern actors and presenters, Graham Norton and Jonathan Ross are flamboyant and outrageous.

We have seen that actors in straight roles go to some lengths to subsume their own personalities into the role that they are playing. There is a branch of show business where, to be successful, you have to do exactly the opposite, and that is stand-up comedy. The solo comedian is performance art at its most extreme, a high-wire act entirely dependent on the skill of a single performer. Consider the challenges. First, the comic has to develop a recognisable persona. If you appeared as someone who wandered in off the street, and tried to keep the audience entertained, you wouldn't last five minutes. Even if

you wanted to appear ordinary, you would have to be extraor-
dinarily ordinary. Something about you, either the appearance,
the delivery or the material, would have to be exaggerated.
Most comics develop some hook, manic like Michael McIntyre,
or deadpan like Jack Dee. And something to separate you from
the hundreds of other comedians, like Ken Dodd with his hair,
or Dame Edna Everage, or early Eddie Izzard with his cross
dressing. Or to take on the men at their own game, like Jo
Brand or Jenny Eclair.

The act has got to be sound, because unlike other performers,
there is no one to help you out. If you are telling one-liners, or
short jokes, then you can get away with the odd duff one, but
generally the act has to stay at a level. And that style of comedy
is incredibly difficult to sustain. Even the best amateur joke
tellers lose their audience after three or four jokes, or about a
quarter of an hour. It was said that Ken Dodd often kept going
for over three hours, his audience crying with laughter all the
while. (He should be knighted.) The other main genre, the
stream of consciousness monologue, is, I should think, even
harder to sustain. It is interesting that the best exponents have
a kind of warmth to their voices – Billy Connolly and Eddie
Izzard spring to mind – which helps them get away with saying
something foul mouthed or outrageous. And the monologue
depends absolutely on continuity. If you lose your thread then
you are gone. I once saw Dylan Moran onstage and, just briefly,
he appeared to stumble over his words. He had taken the
audience with him on his flight of fancy, so we were aware of
this, and there was that moment you can only get in the
theatre, a collective spasm of anxiety. We were willing him to
recover, which he did, but you realised how close it was to
disaster. To put it in perspective, he performed for two hours,
with no other characters to help him out, having to remember
material which was about the length of a play. No wonder they
say it's the loneliest place on earth.

It is no surprise, then, that comedians, especially those who
perform their own material, tend to suffer for their art. The

incidence of mental illness or substance abuse is high in comics, as the well documented lives of some of our famous
performers reveal. Tommy Cooper struggled with alcohol for
much of his career. Tony Hancock also had problems with
alcohol and depression, and committed suicide. Towards the
end of his life he broke with his long-standing collaborators in
a quest to discover 'pure' humour, free from the personalities of
the actors and writers. Russell Brand had substance abuse
issues. Stephen Fry suffers from bipolar disorder or manic
depression. Spike Milligan, perhaps the finest of them all, was
hospitalised several times for manic depression.

Comedians generally display one of the paradoxes of exhibitionism, that this most pure form of public display often
conceals a true nature that is quite the opposite. In a way this is
to be expected – comedians need to be observers rather than
participators to get their material, while the preparation, the
endless hours honing the routine is a solitary occupation. Tests
like the Myers-Briggs Type Indicator have demonstrated that a
surprisingly high percentage of comics prefer introversion, that
is, they mainly get their energy from being alone. Eric More-
cambe was a keen birdwatcher. A more recent study by the
University of New Mexico has shown that, compared to a
control group, comedians are more open to new experiences,
but are less 'agreeable', 'conscientious' and 'extroverted'. In
other words, offstage they are solitary, prickly, and unreliable,
which fits with the descriptions of some of our most famous
names. Spike Milligan was difficult to handle although, 'I told
you I was ill,' was marked on his gravestone, and behind the
joke his illness was the source of much of his comedy. Socrates,
in one of Plato's works, remarks that a sense of the ridiculous is
essential for perspective. In Milligan's case this sense of the
ridiculous pervaded everything he saw, which lead to some
great comedy, but had a devastating effect on him personally.
His humour, though, often contained uncomfortable truths.
Here is the story of a conscript called Neat, in *Adolf Hitler, My*

Part in his Downfall, who kept going absent without leave and was sent to see a psychiatrist:

> 'I don't like the uniform,' Neat told the psychiatrist.
>
> 'And what's wrong with it?'
>
> 'It's dangerous. Germans shoot at it on sight.'

Also, a scene from his novel, *Puckoon*, a joke which still makes me laugh:

> 'Could you spare us a pound?'
>
> 'I've only got a fiver.'
>
> 'It's alright, you can give me the other four later.'

In Milligan's case, the highs were balanced by terrifying lows, when the pain of existence crushed him so much he was almost catatonic. Life at times was genuinely painful for him, and his gift was also a curse that poisoned everything around him.

Much of Spike Milligan's best work was done with actor and comedian Peter Sellers, who is perhaps the most striking example of the perils of dramatic exhibitionism. Sellers was born into an entertainment family and became famous with Milligan in *The Goon Show*. From then on he occupied the artistic stratosphere, making successful films and enjoying the archetypal, much married, friends of the stars, celebrity lifestyle. What made Sellers unique, however, was his willingness to discuss the effect that acting had on him. First, there is his technique for getting into character:

> I start with the voice. Then the face, the makeup ... and then the walk. Very important, the walk. And then,

suddenly something happens. The person takes over. I sink myself into every character I play ... I suddenly know how he is going to react in any given situation.

It is quite clear that 'method' acting came naturally to Sellers. What became increasingly difficult for him was to find his way back to his own personality. Both he and his friends talked candidly about how he was, in effect, always acting, that he had forgotten how 'he' would behave in real life. And Sellers himself admitted that he felt that he 'came alive' when performing, that outside of that he was nothing. This identity crisis cost him a stable and fulfilled private life and, again, led to troubles with mental illness and substance abuse. A surprising number of performers, however, describe a similar feeling, that onstage they are in a completely different state of being. For them, exhibitionism as public display is not for fun, or even fame, it is a *need*.

Most of us think that the ability to be a successful performer is probably restricted to only a small percentage of the population. And we would be right. The famous actor has a visceral need to perform, way beyond any vague stirrings that we might have. They also need self-belief, talent, persistence and luck, of which persistence and self-belief are essential. If you read the biography of most famous actors, they have persisted with their career long after most of us would have thrown in the towel. The person who idly speculates that they would 'love' to be an actor or actress (or, more likely, wants the fame and riches of celebrity) would not even get to first base. It is a lonely and frustrating career, with the two-edged sword of fame awaiting the very few that are successful.

And, even if you do succeed, what do you leave behind? A memory in the minds of your many fans, or perhaps some work on film or DVD, soon to be drowned out by the next big thing? For most actors that would be about it. As Shakespeare put it:

As in a theatre, the eyes of men.
After a well-graced actor leaves the stage,
Are idly bent on him that enters next ...

The performing arts are exhibitionism at its most ephemeral, a career over in a ludicrously short length of time.

Not everyone, however, is content with the fleeting fame that comes with artistic merit. Some people desire a more lasting record of their importance, and wish to leave more than the unreliable memories of performances lost. There is a form of exhibitionism which persists, not just for a few years or even a few centuries, but through millennia. And the legacy it leaves is not an elusive zephyr of memory, but something altogether more concrete. Welcome to the relationship between exhibitionism and power.

6

Exhibitionism and power

In previous chapters we have looked mainly at exhibitionism in individuals, be they sexual deviants, artists or entertainers. We now come to the use of exhibitionism by societies, and the form which is used most frequently to display wealth and power. This type of public display does not register as being particularly exhibitionist, largely because the images are so familiar as to be almost characterless. This does not mean that they are esoteric or difficult to identify, because they are part of the everyday space that we inhabit. It is the use of architecture, or public construction, to display one's self or one's culture.

If you doubt the importance of architecture in the story of exhibitionism, then consider the following: try and name three Roman emperors, and three Roman poets. Now try quoting from one of the poets and name the Roman emperor who conquered Britain. I bet that, like me, you are struggling, and if, like me, you answered 'Julius Caesar' to any of the above then you are wrong. (Julius Caesar invaded Britain, but he was not an Emperor; it was the Emperor Claudius who actually conquered the island in AD43.)

Now I would like you to name two things. First, a famous building in Rome, used for gladiatorial contests. Second, the wall which divides England from Scotland. I expect that you had no trouble identifying the Coliseum and Hadrian's Wall. Even if you had not seen these personally you would still

remember the Romans, because from Hadrian's Wall down to
Exeter there are plenty of physical reminders of their presence.
There is a Roman villa three miles from my home in Glouces-
tershire, and within an hour's drive there are two major Roman
centres, Gloucester and Caerleon. So the Romans are not a
distant, mythical presence, but people who left behind physical remains that we can see and touch. Long-dead writers and
poets and emperors can be ethereal, but the works in brick and
stone endure down the ages.

Their permanence means that they become the iconic symbols of our society. If you were taking children to London you
would want to see the 'sights': the Houses of Parliament, Tower
Bridge, St Paul's Cathedral and Buckingham Palace. The history
of famous civilisations is marked by their buildings, and those
physical remains give us the information that makes them
notable. We know much less about those who built in perish-
able materials like wood, and less still about societies that left
no written record.

Which is not to say that we understand everything about the
iconic constructions of the past: the oldest enduring monument in the world is Stonehenge in Wiltshire, where construction began in about 8000BC. The famous stones were erected
much later, around 3000–2500BC, which still makes them one
of the oldest man-made structures still standing. Of those
buildings that needed excavation, the ziggurats of Ancient
Sumeria, the world's oldest recognised civilisation, date from
around the same time. An astronomical megalith probably
constructed in about 4200BC was discovered at Nabta in the
Sahara desert. The oldest monument constructed in stone was
the step pyramid of Djoser, built in 2650BC. The Pyramids were
built around 2500BC, as was the Sphinx.

It is worth considering for a moment what went into con-
structing these vast structures. One of the circles of Stonehenge
is made up of bluestones, about two metres high and weighing
four tons apiece. The only source for these in modern Britain is
the Preseli Hills in Pembrokeshire, 140 miles away, and the

mystery of how they were transported has still not been solved. They either came by water, but we have no archaeological evidence to support that theory, or they were dragged by land. This is feasible, if you use either a specially constructed cart, or a system of logs as rollers. (The theory that they were magically airlifted by Merlin can, I think, be discounted.) Whichever way they arrived it was going to be highly labour intensive, requiring hundreds, if not thousands of men.

The great trilithons, the horseshoe arrangement of Sarsen stones that are the enduring image of the site, came from the nearby Marlborough Hills. They are about six metres high and weigh a colossal fifty tons each. Sarsens are a dense form of sandstone which is hard to work, especially with the primitive tools of the Neolithic era. The builders of Stonehenge committed their people to a huge, labour-intensive project, which must have reflected its significance as both a symbol and an exhibition of their society.

Although the stone part of Stonehenge was constructed over a period of a thousand years, it is likely that each society who worked on it wanted to construct something complete. As the average human lifespan in 2500BC was less than forty years, it must have meant that the whole society contributed a significant amount of their time to build the monument. Even more remarkably, Stonehenge is only one feature in a landscape littered with prehistoric remains, which includes burial chambers and a wooden henge. The individual features are linked by ancient track ways, which could be processional routes. Although nobody really knows the purpose of these monuments, it is likely that the area is a ritual landscape, representing a journey from life to death. It was clearly known throughout the prehistoric world, as archaeology shows that it attracted people from all over Britain and the continent. Clearly the need to exhibit one's culture by building was an early marker of civilisation.

The other great structures of the time were found in Egypt – the Pyramids of Giza and the Sphinx. The Great Pyramid was made from limestone blocks, with granite used for the King's Chamber, and polished limestone used to 'face' the exterior. The limestone was cut from a nearby quarry, while the granite was transported from Aswan, 500 miles away down the Nile. The archaeologist John Romer estimated that it took 14 years to build the Great Pyramid, requiring two gangs of 100,000 men apiece. The pyramid is carefully constructed, with a King and Queens's chamber, a gallery, and shafts leading to the outside.

We know that it was built as a mausoleum for the Pharaoh Khufu. What has astonished modern archaeologists and architects is the precision of the building. The sides of the base are 756 feet long and they have a mean deviation of just two and a half *inches*. That would be a remarkable feat for modern engineering, let alone for a building erected nearly 5000 years ago. There are other mathematical curiosities in the building measurements, like the ratio of the perimeter to the height of the building, which is two pi, pi being the ratio of a circle's circumference to its diameter. These and other measurements have sparked a host of theories about the significance of the building and its relationship with forgotten, or still secret, societies. It is claimed that the pyramid shape can 'preserve' food, and will keep razor blades sharp. The alignment of the three pyramids is thought to mirror the constellation of Orion, and if one recreates the night sky of 2,500BC, then one of the shafts of the Great Pyramid points straight at Sirius.

Conspiracy and alien theories aside, one cannot doubt how majestic the pyramid must have looked, tall, perfectly symmetrical, and clothed in white limestone. Two thousand years later, the Greek traveller and poet Antipater listed it as one of the Seven Wonders of the World. The original translation named them as 'seven things to be seen', the Greek words for 'sight' and 'wonder' being very similar. In a classical world full of beautiful buildings and structures these must have been especially impressive to warrant listing. And it is indicative of mankind's veneration of architecture that they were constructions, rather than, say, plays or athletic games. The Seven Wonders were, in chronological order:

- The Pyramids 2560BC
- The Hanging Gardens of Babylon 600BC
- The Temple of Artemis at Ephesus 550BC
- The Statue of Zeus at Olympia 450BC
- The Mausoleum at Halicarnassus 352BC
- The Colossus of Rhodes 292BC
- The Lighthouse at Alexandria 280BC

Antipater considered the Temple of Artemis to be the most impressive of the wonders. It was 450 feet long, 225 feet wide and 60 feet high, which compares favourably with St Paul's Cathedral at 518 feet long, and 121 feet wide, although its dome makes St Paul's higher. It was still a wonderful feat of design and engineering. Of the Wonders, only the Pyramids remain intact, although all the others are verifiable from remains, with the possible exception of the Colossus of Rhodes. It is interesting to note their purpose: two are tombs, the Mausoleum and the Pyramids; one is a Temple; two are statues, Zeus and the Colossus; one is a lighthouse; and the Hanging Gardens were a present, built by a king for his home-sick wife. The site of the last, Babylon, also had another wonder, walls so thick that a chariot could be ridden around the battlements. Their size and complexity was the clearest indication of a society's wealth and power, and is exhibitionism at its most straightforward.

The first great European builders were the Greeks, and they were responsible for five of the seven wonders. It is interesting that the most iconic Greek building today, the Parthenon in Athens, was not considered to be a Wonder, probably because it is only half the size of the Temple of Artemis, at 228 feet long, 101 feet wide, and 45 feet high. When we come to architecture as public display, size matters. Wonder or not, the Parthenon remains the symbol of the Golden Age of Greek architecture between the sixth and fifth centuriesBC. 'The art of the Age of Pericles,' wrote the architect Sir Reginald Blomfield, 'is the fountainhead to which all artists return.' Modern architects and engineers still marvel at the precision of the Parthenon, and the imagination which could conceive of such a feat. It is, according to the nineteenth century French architect Auguste Choisey, 'the supreme effort of genius in the pursuit of beauty'. Although Ancient Greek theatre, science, medicine, philosophy and politics are all templates of genius, the fixed points of their culture are their buildings. We can see the Parthenon, we know it is a work of genius, and from that everything else flows.

The Greek style of architecture was distributed around the Mediterranean and Near East in the wake of Alexander's conquests, and has left us a rich legacy of theatres and temples. When we think of classical architecture and the construction of memorable buildings, however, we think primarily of Rome. And although we think of Rome in terms of an Empire, it is important to realise that it started life as a kingdom, a Mediterranean city-state. It was a republic before Julius Caesar became its dictator, and his successor Augustus the first emperor.

The rise of Augustus is an interesting story of the acquisition of power. He had been named as the heir to his great uncle, the childless Julius Caesar, whose political machinations had left behind a state of unrest. Octavian, as Augustus was then known, formed a triumvirate with Anthony and Pompeius to rule Rome. This was always likely to be unstable in the febrile atmosphere of pre-Imperial Rome, and the factions provoked a civil war. Octavian defeated both Pompeius and Anthony in separate campaigns, the latter in the battle of Actium, after which Anthony and his lover Cleopatra committed suicide. His military victories, control of the army, wealth, and network of political contacts granted him an unassailable position. At the invitation of the Senate, Octavian became the Emperor Augustus. Ruthless men seize power; great men create the circumstances for it to be offered as a gift.

We associate Imperial Rome with the great buildings, but some of the most important, like the Forum and the Circus Maximus, actually predated the Empire. This pre-Imperial Rome had grown organically and was somewhat haphazard. Emperor Augustus brought order to the city, refashioning the forum and adding many new buildings as well as refurbishing the old. He built the Temple of Caesar, the Baths of Agrippa and the temple of Mars Ultor in the Forum. He allegedly said on his deathbed: 'I found a city of bricks; I have left you one of marble'. Although by 200BC Rome had conquered Italy, the Adriatic coastline, and part of Spain, its empire became established from the time of Julius Caesar onwards. At its height around AD500 it extended from Britain in the West to Turkey and Syria in the East, incorporating some of Germany in the North and the North African coastline in the South. Wherever they went, the Romans left behind concrete reminders of their power and engineering skill in the form of temples, aqueducts, villas, forts and roads. We know they had an empire because we can see its remains. This lesson has not been lost on the powerful down the ages.

The Romans were adept at building to display might, one of the first manifestations being the triumphal arch. They were used to celebrate the victories of generals, or the founding of new colonies. The building of arches predated the empire, but after Augustus only the emperor was allowed to be commemorated in such a way. There were originally 36 such arches in Rome, but only three have survived: the arches of Titus, Severus, and Constantine. The building of an arch to commemorate military victory was still practised up to the nineteenth century with the construction of the Arc de Triomphe in Paris, built by Napoleon, and Wellington's Arch in London. Pliny the Elder, writing in the first century AD, detected the egotism behind such projects, believing that the arch, 'elevated (the person) above the ordinary world'.

Outstanding military victory was celebrated with a 'triumph', in which the victorious general would be led into Rome by the senate, leading his army, and with captives in cages or chains. It was a religious and civil ceremony – bulls were sacrificed and the captives publicly executed. To be awarded a triumph it was necessary to win a war, or fight a battle in which over 5,000 men were killed. The awarding of a triumph could be dangerous both for the victorious general and the senate by creating a popular public figure capable of challenging for power. Partly because of this, the emperors forbade the awarding of a triumph to anyone but themselves.

The Roman Emperors also understood the need to cement their power by retaining the support of the population, which led to building of Rome's most iconic landmark, the Colosseum. It was completed in about AD80 by the Emperor Titus, and was used to stage gladiatorial contests, re-enact famous battles, animal hunts and even sea battles. It was capable of seating 50,000 spectators, making it comparable to a modern football stadium. The population needed only 'bread and circuses' according to the poet Juvenal, meaning that if one could keep people fed and entertained, then they would refrain from considering deeper questions about the nature of their governance. Like many structures from past, the Colosseum is symbolic of the mysterious nature of power. The name has an interesting provenance, because the amphitheatre was called after the nearby Colossus of Nero, a 30 metre high bronze statue of the infamous violin-playing Emperor. It is said that Nero actually set fire to the city himself to clear a space for his own building projects.

It would be quite wrong, however, to suggest that the Roman architects were concerned solely with representing Imperial power. The Romans understood the need to build *as* public display and *for* public display. There is considerable beauty in their buildings, and also technical skill amounting to genius. The Romans invented the arch, and the dome, and it would be many centuries before those skills would be rediscovered. As Christianity spread in the later empire, churches were modelled on the Roman basilica, buildings with a central nave flanked by aisles and a curved or apsidal east end. This style of architecture, known as Romanesque, became popular throughout Europe, surviving the disintegration of the empire. Many of our cathedrals are based on this style, which in Britain we more commonly call Norman.

This brings us to the second, and last, conquest of England by a foreign power, the Norman invasion of 1066. Like the Romans, the Normans had to establish control over the countryside by establishing a series of strongpoints where they could base sufficient force to subdue the native population. In the first 20 years of William's reign, an astonishing 500 castles were constructed, ranging from simple motte and bailey (moat and single tower) works to great edifices like Warwick Castle and the Tower of London. Even more impressive, at least 90 of these castles are still standing. Like the Romans, we know that the Normans were here because we can see their legacy.

Today we may wonder why the Normans went to such lengths to conquer and subdue England. The answer is, quite simply, for the land, and the money and power that such a conquest would bring. In the Middle Ages, wool, grain, crops and cattle were the sources of profit, and the more land you owned, the richer you were likely to be. It was impossible for William to control England from London, so the system of castles became the bases for the Normans to control the country. The Normans had only 10,000 men to subdue this native population of two million, some of whom, like the remnants of the Vikings, Danes, and the native Saxons, were bellicose in the extreme. The number of castles, and the short distances in between, meant the Norman lords could deal with insurrection very quickly.

Their power was also displayed in the construction of the great abbeys and churches of England. For many of the population these were the most accessible Norman buildings, and they must have regarded them with something like awe. To go from the wattle and daub dwellings of our towns into the nave of a Norman abbey, with its great stone columns, carved arches, and high ceilings, must have been a religious experience in itself. The churches and abbeys were the cultural, as well as spiritual, centres of medieval life, reflected in the architectural innovations of the Middle Ages. Norman, or Romanesque, architecture was followed by Gothic, and then early English decorated and perpendicular styles. The latter was particularly impressive, the great windows filling the building with light, and the straight lines of the masonry drawing the eye to Heaven. The two great powers of the Middle Ages, the Royal Houses and the Catholic Church, left their mark in stone.

They also chose other ways to exhibit power. William the Conqueror publicly wore his crown three times a year at Gloucester, Winchester and Westminster. In that way he became 'real', the people could see him as their indisputable ruler. This was important, because the thread of rebellion and usurpation runs right through the tangled history of England. An invisible king was a mythical king, and open to challenge if the circumstances were right.

Rebellion had to be dealt with swiftly and publicly. In the reign of Henry III, the penalty for treason was 'hanging, drawing and quartering', a public execution of the utmost cruelty. The victim was tied to a wooden panel, hung until nearly dead, disembowelled (while still alive) and beheaded. The body was then divided up into four parts, and these were publicly displayed, sometimes even being transported around the country. As medieval courts were full of intrigue, with spies and informers everywhere, it meant that the potential rebel had to be very careful indeed. Punishments for all sorts of crimes were carried out in public, and were often very popular – hangings attracted huge crowds well into the nineteenth century. Public execution was very important in the relationship between exhibitionism and power, as there is no greater display of might than to publicly kill your opponent. We are reminded of this whenever we see the image of Christ crucified. We may believe that the Western world has moved on, but think of the deaths of

Saddam Hussain and Osama Bin Laden and ask, has anything much really changed?

The use of building to display ecclesiastical power in the Middle Ages reached its zenith with the construction of St Peter's Basilica in Rome, at the heart of the Vatican. It was designed by the Italian architect Donate Bramante in 1503 and modified by several other architects, including Michelangelo. The whole complex was finished in 1626. Although we know the names of previous 'architects', mainly builder abbots like Serlo in Gloucester, it is after the Italian Renaissance that the discipline becomes established. The earliest famous British architect is Inigo Jones, who built the Banqueting House in Whitehall and remodelled Covent Garden. Like many of his contemporaries he was influenced by the writings of the Italian architect Andrea Palladio, whose style leaned heavily on Ancient Greece and Rome.

By the time Jones was working, England had become a major trading power, with colonies in North America and the West Indies. A newly wealthy mercantile class were created, the bourgeoisie, the middle class, existing somewhere between the working class, the nobility, and the clergy. They displayed their creativity in making money, and displayed their wealth in bricks and mortar. Great buildings were no longer the sole preserve of the nobility and the Church but the ordinary, albeit rich, private citizen. Architect designed English country houses first appeared in the Elizabethan Age, and the next two centuries saw English domestic architecture change dramatically. The new mansions were unfortified, and typically Palladian in style, the entrances framed with classical columns. Examples include Hampton Court Palace, Kedleston Hall in Derby, built by the Curzon family, and Holkham Hall in Norfolk. The great houses were built to display wealth, and as suitable places to entertain the eminent citizens of their time. In an offshoot of this work, the eighteenth century saw the gentry landscape their gardens, most famously under the direction of Lancelot 'Capability' Brown. In a very English form of exhibitionism, these great landscaped gardens were often dotted with eccentric buildings, or follies, built for pleasure or display. A favourite folly was the miniature classical temple, although towers, monuments, pagodas, mock ruins, and even a house with a pineapple on the roof, can be found in the gardens of Britain. An obelisk built like a bayonet was erected on the Blackdown Hills in Somerset to commemorate Wellington's victory at Waterloo.

The Great Fire of London in 1666 destroyed much of the old city, but out of the ashes came one of England's iconic buildings, St Paul's Cathedral. Designed by Sir Christopher Wren, and built in a style known as English baroque, St Paul's was completed in 1697, making it a relative newcomer in the history of Britain's cathedrals. The cathedral with its dome was modelled partially on St Peter's in the Vatican, reflecting the ability of architecture to cross boundaries more completely than any other artistic discipline. Although it is one of Britain's landmark buildings it occupies a curious place both architecturally and emotionally in the narrative of our nation. The writer and critic Jonathan Meades explains why:

> Of London's major set pieces St Paul's Cathedral is the most distinguished, though not, I suspect, the most loved; it is too stately, aloof and worldly to excite the sort of affection granted to such exercises in quaintness as Big Ben or Tower Bridge. It is a marvellously protean building: classified as baroque but too temperate, northern and humanely restrained to share that name with the inebriated swirling stones of Bavaria and Sicily; a temple that wears the vestments of Rome and the Counter-Reformation yet could never be taken for anything other than Protestant; a treasure house of sublime craftsmanship to amble through and a uniquely bold landmark from countless distant vantage points.

Architecture is the surest way, in the West, of displaying not just wealth, but also civilised culture. The White House, home to the President of the United States of America, has an entrance framed by pillars in the classical style. The Senate building also has a classical pillared façade, and is topped with a dome. In nearly every major Western city you will find buildings modelled in the Greek and Roman style, their entrances a series of columns holding up an elaborately decorated triangular lintel. Building in the classical style is not just plain imitation, but is a statement of a society's aspirations. 'Look at us,' it says, 'we are on a par with Ancient Greek and Rome.' The idea of the classical world as the zenith of human civilisation persisted well into the nineteenth century, a remarkable achievement. To create a whole new style of architecture is one thing, but for that style to remain a template for two millennia is quite another, an enduring testimony to a society's genius.

The need to build is related both to power and to the individual's opinion of his or her position in the world. Occasionally the two coincide in reality, as in the case of Louis XIV, the fabled Sun King, who ruled France from 1638 to 1715. Louis built Europe's grandest residence, the palace of Versailles, which covers over 2000 acres. It is still the largest residence built for a royal family in the world. It was big enough to house the nobility of France, who were encouraged to pay court to the Sun King. The palace ran on a Byzantine court ritual, which had Louis at the centre of household activity. Here Louis could control his rivals and thus maintain his power. Even their mail was intercepted to check for signs of nascent conspiracies. Louis was an absolute monarch, descended from a long line of kings, ruler by divine right, and his hold over his country was absolute. Yet he was in many respects insecure, being susceptible to flattery, and probably over-fond of the glory of war. Versailles is a symptom of that insecurity, being massive and somewhat pompous in its execution. Louis' desire for recognition, not only to *be* the most powerful man in the world, but to *be seen to be* the most powerful man in the world would lead modern psychologists to suspect a personality disorder. This combination of egotism and supreme power sowed the seeds of the French Revolution, in which the masses dissolved the nobility and the church.

The European nations of the eighteenth and nineteenth centuries were the most powerful countries in the world and spent much of that time adding other nations to their empires. By 1886 Britain had the largest empire the world had ever seen, encompassing Canada, Australia, New Zealand, the whole of India, parts of Africa, and the West Indies. The acquisition of all this territory, and the raw materials and produce this entailed, made Britain fabulously wealthy. Just like the Romans and the Normans before us, we left our mark on the colonies in their infrastructure. Britain built the fourth largest railway system in the world in India, and completely rebuilt cities like Mumbai (Bombay). Indian cities gained Victorian municipal and administrative buildings and Gothic churches. Later, Indian styles were merged with Western to produce something altogether unique. The Victoria railway terminal in Mumbai, now the Chhatrapati Shivaji Terminus, is an example of this architectural genetic engineering, encompassing Victorian Italianate Gothic, and leavened with traditional Indian adornments. The result is something familiar yet disturbing; St Pancras crossed with the Taj Mahal. It remains the largest railway terminus in the world, and is a UNESCO World Heritage Site. It is a beautiful, if unique, building, but its creation, and the railway system it symbolised, owed more to military pragmatism and the need, after the Indian Mutiny, to get troops quickly to any trouble spot.

Like the Romans and the Normans, we also left an administrative and intellectual legacy that persists to the present day, and which gained the admiration of some native Indians, like the writer Nirad Chaudhuri. But there was a cruel side to empire, and ruthless exploitation, something we in Britain have downplayed in our magisterial histories. One of the great writers of the twentieth century, George Orwell, left an account of the empire from a sceptic's point of view in his novel *Burmese*

Days, and in other writing on his days as a policeman in Burma. This depicts the empire as a grubby conspiracy, where many are exploited to make profits for a few. Orwell reflects candidly on his own mixed feelings about both his job as a policeman, and his relationship with the natives. The eccentricities of the British, however, could not be entirely quashed by the demands of empire – two of our legacies are cricket and bell ringing, often held up as examples of our civilising mission to the colonies.

While Britain was busy acquiring an empire, living conditions in our towns and rapidly expanding cities had not much changed since the Middle Ages. Not to put too fine a point on it, they stank. The streets were still awash with faeces, both animal and human, and water was supplied by street pumps which drew on contaminated sources. Typhoid and cholera were rife. The Thames was little more than an open sewer, and the stench was overpowering, so much so that in 1858 London almost came to a standstill. Plans were even considered to move some of the important centres of Government, including Parliament and the Law Courts, out into the cleaner suburbs. It was after this 'great stink' of 1858 that Parliament recognised the scale of the problem and commissioned Joseph Bazalgette to construct a system of sewers. Although no one could consider a sewer as a work of exhibitionism, a complex of public works which include the proper disposal of waste and the provision of clean water probably makes more impact on a person's environment than the most visually appealing building project. Exhibitionism and public display is often an end in itself, but more often there is a purpose to the project. A comedian demonstrates that he can make you laugh, an architect that he can create a beautiful building, and a civil engineer that he can improve our living environment. London ceased to smell, proving that the absence of something is a form of public display in itself. Bazalgette's sewerage system was named as one of the Seven Wonders of the Industrial World in a 2003 BBC documentary series. The other six were:

- The Great Ship – the Great Eastern, built by Isambard Kingdom Brunel in 1858
- Brooklyn Bridge in New York, built by the Roebling family, opened in 1883
- The Bell Rock Lighthouse off the coast of Scotland, built by Robert Stephenson (grandfather of the author Robert Louis Stevenson), completed in 1810
- The Panama Canal, begun in 1881 by a French engineer, Ferdinand de Lesseps, and finished by a series of American engineers in 1914
- The Line – the Pacific Railroad. This was the first transcontinental railway line, which owed its genesis to successive Pacific Railroad acts passed in Congress. Built in the 1860s, the most notable early sponsors were Asa Whitney and Theodore Judah. Several companies were involved in its construction.
- The Hoover Dam. Named after the President of the United States Herbert Hoover, who had commissioned the work when Secretary for Commerce. It was built between 1931 and 1936 by a consortium of companies. It was designed by John L. Savage, and the construction supervised by the renowned dam builder Frank Crowe.

Shortly after the transformation of London, another revolution was happening in America. In 1884, a building ten stories high was constructed in Chicago, the Home Insurance Building. Although not considered a skyscraper by modern standards, it was the first building to use a steel frame construction, an innovation which enabled architects to build 'up'. The second was the invention of the safety elevator by Elisha Otis, which enabled people to move easily between floors. These two developments revolutionised construction, and the appearance of Western cities was transformed. It also signified the emergence of the USA as a global player, indicating once again the relationship between construction and power. The first all steel skyscraper was the Rand-McNally building in Chicago, and the prototype straight sided office building, the Wainwright Building in St Louis.

The appearance of skyscrapers reflected a more pronounced shift in the distribution of power and wealth in society. These new monuments were built not by kings or religions but by companies. The Rand-McNally housed publishers, and the Wainwright a brewing company. The most iconic skyscraper of them all, the Empire State Building, built in 1931, was occupied by offices and broadcasting stations.

The emergence of the skyscraper was also symbolic of the industrial age, the essential component being the steel necessary to frame the building. Although steel had been made for hundreds of years, it was only produced in industrial quantities after Henry Bessemer invented his smelting process in 1858. The previous limitation on the height of buildings was the difficulties inherent in stone or brick construction. If you build by cementing one stone or brick on top of another, after a certain height, probably around two stories, the structure becomes unstable. One can get round this by widening the base, but even then you cannot build up to much more than about 300 feet. The great spires of our cathedrals were the best example of this, although the medieval builders required several attempts to get it right. The current tower at Gloucester Cathedral is probably the third or fourth on the site, rising over 200 feet, and containing 6,000 tons of stone.

Framing a building in steel solves this problem, but even then there is a limit to the height, mainly due to the sheer quantity of material involved. In the 1960s a young Bangladeshi–American engineer called Fazlur Khan invented the tubular design system, which was structurally more stable and also cut building costs. This sparked the current explosion of high-rise buildings in our towns and cities. The Empire State Building was the tallest building in the world at 1,250 feet, until 1972, when it was overtaken by the twin towers of the World Trade Center. These were rapidly overtaken by the Sears Tower in Chicago, built by Khan, which at 1,450 feet stayed as the tallest building in the world until 1998. The current tallest building in the world is the Burj Khalifa, a complex of homes, offices and hotels that rises to 2,723 feet from the centre of Dubai. Just as the skyscraper signified the USA's rise to economic prominence, so the global movement of money can be tracked by the appearance of new skyscrapers in the cities of the Far East, Middle East, Russia, India, and Brazil. Fazlur Khan has probably had more influence on the built environment than any other man in history, and the rich and powerful have plundered his invention in a frenzy to exhibit their importance. It is also not difficult to draw psychological parallels between a certain part of the male anatomy and the shape of the various skyscrapers dotted around the world. Exhibitionism moves in mysterious ways.

Architecture is often considered as a form of art, and like art it explored new directions in the twentieth century. The Bauhaus movement in Germany even went as far as to claim that, 'the ultimate aim of all creativity is building'. The mechanics of building changed with the new materials, and a new generation of architects experimented with shape and form. The Bauhaus architects Walter Gropius and Adolf Meyer used steel and glass to produce functional buildings, the best example being the Bauhaus college in Dessau. The block-like buildings three or four stories high became a model for public buildings throughout the world. The Bauhaus movement extended into art and crafts, and was politically left wing. Hitler closed it down in 1933.

An associate of the Bauhaus movement was Mies van der Rohe, an architect who pioneered a minimalist approach creating free flowing spaces. He wanted his architecture to be symbolic of his time, a reflection of the new technological and industrial age. His design 'Brick Country House' radically altered the concept of domestic space, containing freestanding walls that do not form rooms. The interior space is therefore fluid, an effect that should be liberating but is actually disturbing. Van der Rohe moved to America, where he designed more formal large buildings. One of these was the famous Seagram building, a skyscraper on Park Avenue, New York, which Mies had set back from the road, creating a plaza in the front of the building. He also clad the skeleton of the building with bronze coloured beams, making it dark, almost black, in its appearance. These two innovations, much criticised at the time, were widely copied in later constructions. Every cityscape in the world now has its dark tower.

A contemporary of Mies was Le Corbusier, a French architect and intellectual, who, like Mies, radically rethought the concept of interior space. His philosophy is best seen in the Villa Savoye, which expresses Corbusier's 'five points' of architecture. First, the house is built on stilts, avoiding the need for load bearing walls. This led to the second point, a free flowing façade, and the third, an open plan floor space. The fourth point was the use of large ribbon windows, and the fifth the presence of a roof garden. 'Corb', as he was known, did not however, stop there, but produced plans for redesigning whole cities. One of his ideas, which spread to most of the cities in the world, was the use of high-rise buildings to house people, especially the urban poor. His designs were accused of being sterile, and turning inner cities into impersonal aggregations of steel and glass.

This was borne out by the experience in inner city Britain. The 1960s saw a boom in the construction of the housing tower block, seen at the time as a utopian solution to the problem of social housing in urban areas. Unfortunately they rapidly became dystopias, the anonymous public spaces and dimly lit stairwells encouraging vandalism and crime. A collective psychosis seemed to grip town planners in post-war Britain, as they ripped the heart out of our communities and replaced diversity with brutalism. In many respects twentieth century architecture was a straight reflection of the dominant ideologies of that dangerous century. Capitalism gave us the corporate palaces reaching for the sky, where human beings were reduced to the status of ants, and Communism elevated functionalism to an art, housing its people in drab, soulless slabs of concrete. Architecture has always been political, but often actively confined only to a small group of producers and consumers. In the twentieth century, it began to affect everyone.

At the upper end of the scale, celebrity architects, like artists, began to experiment with exotic and innovative aspects of their craft. This could be radical in the extreme, like the Lloyds Building in London, designed by Richard Rogers. His innovation was to put elevators, electrical systems and water pipes on the outside of the structure, leading it to be dubbed the 'inside out' building. In a sort of rite of passage the building was, at first, vilified, before becoming a national treasure. The postwar years may have seen a revolution in architecture, but it also ushered in an open season on architects. A proposed extension to the National Gallery was attacked by the Prince of Wales as a 'monstrous carbuncle', and virtually every building put up in London since then has been criticised. Which is understandable because of all the forms of exhibitionism, construction is the most enduring. You can walk away from a painting, and leave a concert hall, but it is hard to ignore some great lump of steel and glass outside your bedroom window. There is a certain arrogance in this need to dominate the eye line, especially as most of the buildings are offices, and off limits to the general public. Ordinary people respond by bringing these palaces of the new global capitalism down to earth with sarcastic nicknames. London has the Gherkin, the Cheesegrater, Ken's (now Boris's) Testicle, and the Shard, with the Can of Ham to come. Exhibitions of superiority can rapidly become objects of ridicule.

The buildings and public constructions are part of our society, and they can become symbols of our society, associated with the sense of nationhood. When Saddam Hussain ruled Iraq, his cult of personality saw his statue adorn public spaces, with his face displayed on every public building. One of the most enduring images of his fall was of soldiers and civilians pulling down his statue in Bhagdad's Firdos Square. Destruction of a regime's symbols signifies the transfer of power.

Or, in that case, did it? It was hailed as the end of the war in Iraq, yet in reality, it was only the tentative end of the Battle for Bagdhad. The actual war had many more years to run. Yet the image of that statue being pulled down remains for many of us, me included, the enduring symbol of that war. And the cheering of the crowd, who we thought were mainly Iraqi's, helped to legitimise the conflict in the eyes of many who doubted the decision to invade. Yet it now turns out that there were, at most, a few hundred people there, and a sizeable proportion of those were servicemen or journalists.

So that image, which we have come to believe as a defining moment in the history of the war, and an affirmation of grassroots Iraqi support for the invasion, turns out to be neither. Exhibitionism is not often a moral activity.

Destruction, and its companion looting, are perennial exhibitions of mankind's endless capacity for conflict. One of the most notorious incidences of this occurred in 1860, in Beijing, China, during the second Opium War. A party of British and French officers and soldiers went under a flag of truce to negotiate with the Chinese. They were captured, and some were tortured and murdered. When their corpses were found by the rest of the army they had been mutilated so badly that they were barely recognisable. Their discovery provoked a mood of simmering anger in the invading British and French armies. Beijing contained the emperor's Old Summer Palace, a combination of nature and art so perfect that it was considered to be the equal of any of the ancient Wonders of the World. This huge complex, eight times the size of Vatican City, contained paintings, gardens temples lakes and bridges, all meticulously coordinated. It was said that in some of the views, it was difficult to see where human painting left off and real nature began. The buildings were full of precious silks, jewels, gold and pottery.

The response of the invaders to the torture of their fellows was to loot and destroy the Summer Palace completely. Centuries of painstaking craftsmanship, one of the great works of human artistic endeavour, was erased in less than a week. This was not, however, just an attack of wanton barbarianism, but a deliberate attempt to send a message to China's rulers that torture would not be tolerated. We punished their baser instincts by destroying their highest achievement. It was a brutal lesson in exhibiting power, which still carries an aura of shame 150 years later.

Up until the new millennium, we may have thought that the civilised world was immune from such barbarity. Then came 9/11, when a group of Al Qaeda suicide bombers hijacked four planes and flew them into targets in America. It is significant that they chose iconic buildings as their targets. The twin towers of the World Trade Center dominated the skyline of New York, the Pentagon was the heart of America's military and intelligence systems, and the Senate building the centre of government. Their destruction could hardly send a more powerful message to the world about Al Qaeda's own power, and their ability to strike anywhere. As we know, the twin towers were destroyed, the Pentagon badly damaged, and the plane destined for the Senate was brought down by the heroic acts of its passengers. This was exhibitionism as an epoch-defining act, a public display of hatred that has led to a decade of conflict. If building is a statement of power, skill, and wealth, then its destruction is equally symbolic for the aggressors. The attackers knew that the power of the Western media, its ability to beam this public display around the world, would ensure the maximum publicity for this atrocity. With the rise of the global media, the creation of supranational corporations, and the all pervasive influence of the internet, these acts could not be hidden or minimised.

This is also a two way process. Exhibitionism and extravagant display was once the preserve of a select few. That is no longer true. If you want to exhibit something nowadays then the world is at your fingertips. And what is surprising is that ordinary people, who not so long ago led largely unexamined lives, have embraced it with considerable vigour. We are in the digital age, and have entered a wholly new era in relationships with interconnectedness and social media. Millions of people now share intimate details of their lives with friends and casual acquaintances, and even more bizarrely, *people that they will never meet*. And even those who don't want to splash their lives all over the net are still revealing themselves simply through the sites they visit on their computer. Like it or not, exhibitionism has gone global, for private individuals as well as celebrities. But who or what is it that we are exhibiting?

7

Exhibitionism in the modern world

Exhibitionism, or to be more precise, extravagant public display, has undergone a revolution in the past fifty years. For most of the twentieth century, exhibitionism was either a somewhat laughable sexual activity, or a performance confined to the margins of show business. Both were not part of mainstream society, and it would have been possible to live comfortably without encountering either on a regular basis. Perhaps more importantly, exhibitionism, or 'showing off', was considered to be a character defect, particularly unacceptable in young people.

This is, however, no longer true. There are now so many outlets for exhibitionism, and so many new variants of exhibitionist behaviour, that it is hardly possible to avoid it. Even more remarkably, exhibitionism, previously thought to be socially undesirable, has become tolerated, and even admired. So what has caused this transition from disapproval to respectability?

To answer the question, we need to compare the social attitudes of post-war Britain with the world of the twenty-first century. The poet Phillip Larkin is credited with announcing the start of the modern era in his poem 'Annus Mirabilis':

Sexual intercourse began
In nineteen sixty-three
(Which was rather late for me)
Between the end of the Chatterley ban
And the Beatles' first LP.

The poem is important because Larkin is acknowledging the moment when moral attitudes in Britain began to change. Britain in the years after the Second World War was a tired, drab, country where everyone knew their place, and where there were unspoken, and rigid, codes of behaviour. This society was formal, regimented, dull, and no place for the young, who wanted a little more excitement in their lives. The inevitable reaction resulted in the social revolution dubbed the 'swinging sixties', which changed the position of the individual in society more profoundly than anything that had gone before. To understand the magnitude of the change, and the associated rise of exhibitionism, we need to look more closely at that austere world of 1950s Britain.

The defining factor of society in fifties Britain was that everyone 'knew their place'. The class system was largely intact, with quite delineated 'upper', 'middle', and 'lower' or 'working' classes. The upper Classes were the monarchy, hereditary landowners, and the upper ranks of the professions. The middle classes were the professionals; doctors, teachers, bank managers, and owners of businesses. The working class were the manual labourers and factory workers. By and large, each class kept to themselves, and lived and socialised together in almost separate communities. There was little movement between classes and each of them, especially the upper and working class, could spot an outsider a mile off. The upper classes had a set of social criteria which were largely unspoken, but encompassed every form of behaviour from speech to dress to conduct at the dinner table. The working class similarly had a set of unspoken rules, although not as comprehensive, which hinged around contempt for people who were either patronising or pretending that they were from humble origins. The middle classes strived to maintain their distance from the working class while simultaneously trying, and failing, to join the upper class. Within these three main groups there were numerous subgroups, all with their unspoken inclusions and exclusions, creating a system so complex that it made the fabulously intricate court of Byzantium look like a model of simplicity.

One example can be found in the use of vocabulary, which the writer Nancy Mitford divided into U (upper class) language, as used by the nobility, and Non-U, that used by everyone else. So, the quality would refer to a 'lavatory', (with a long second 'a', naturally), and the hoi polloi, a 'toilet'. The upper classes would use a napkin at luncheon, the lower orders a serviette at tea, and they would retire to their drawing room or lounge respectably. The social climber, or 'parvenu', was only a slip of the tongue away from social oblivion. It was a world that was almost psychopathic in its complexity and lack of empathy. There are still echoes of it today – the Mayor of London, Boris Johnson, educated at Eton and Oxford, is often described as an 'outsider' by Tory grandees, an opinion which is absolutely mystifying to the rest of Britain. Eton ... Oxford ... plummy voice ... rich ... and you say he's one of us? Hmmm.

It was not just the use of vocabulary that separated the classes. The accent of your voice, and the use of correct tenses were important. The upper classes spoke clearly in rich tones with impeccable grammar, whereas the lower classes spoke in dialect and often mixed their tenses – 'the boy done good' and so on. To speak with a regional accent was to label oneself as a country bumpkin and therefore, by definition, thick as a brick. At my school in Cornwall in the 1960s we had an English mistress who tried desperately to get us yokels to speak properly, an experiment which met with as much success as Canute's attempts to turn back the tide.

You would not have to wait until the person spoke, however, to place them socially. The classes dressed differently. The upper classes favoured tailored three-piece suits, and those who worked in the civil service, finance, and the law often wore a form of morning dress, complete with bowler hat. The middle classes similarly favoured suits or jacket and tie, while the working class would wear their work clothes, which were often of fairly rough, shapeless material. The working class would only wear a suit on special occasions, or on a Sunday to go to church or chapel. Children were similarly dressed up for special occasions. We wore ordinary clothes to primary school, and you could tell a poor family by the state of those clothes. You could also tell a poor family by their smell, as heating water was an expensive business in those days and the domestic shower had not been invented. Even a middle class family like mine would only bathe twice a week.

The communities we lived in were stable, enclosed, and often claustrophobic. Transport was very limited, most families not owning a car, which meant you rarely left your town or village. I grew up in a town called Looe, in Cornwall, and we only left there once a week to visit relatives in St Austell, 25 miles away. It was as if the counties themselves were a series of little kingdoms, interconnected yet mutually exclusive. The lack of transport meant that Looe was entirely self-contained, with butchers, tailors, greengrocers, shoe shops and grocers all within walking distance. The population was largely stable, with interconnected families who went back generations. Divorce was virtually unheard of and most of my friends grew up in families where only one parent, usually the father, went out to work. This created a closed community where everyone knew everyone else. You knew very little of the wider world.

It sounds idyllic, but it could be claustrophobic. In the fifties and early sixties there were definite ideas about how you should behave – speak properly, be polite, stand up straight, say 'please' and 'thank you', keep your hands out of your pockets and respect your elders. And don't behave irresponsibly, or be a nuisance to anyone. Any lapse from these standards was usually noted instantly. I remember returning home one evening after cycling around the town with my friends to find my father looking stern. 'What's this you've been up to?' he asked, and when I feigned ignorance he told me that I had been spotted cycling carelessly on the road near the police station. And that was it –just a bit of bad cycling which caused a car to brake a bit suddenly. It was like living in a benign police state.

One of the worst crimes you could commit was to be thought of as a 'show off', someone who was constantly drawing attention to themselves. In the intricate, introverted world of post war Britain, this applied as much to adults as to children. Any deviation from what was expected of you would be frowned on. For example, I remember a friend of my father's splashing out on a new and rather 'flash' car. He may have thought it was something to be admired, but his friends subtly and inexorably mocked it until the poor man finally gave in and went back to his Morris Minor. It sounds cruel, and it probably was, but it reflected people's desire for stability, that you shouldn't get ideas 'above your station'. I should add, paradoxically, that in Cornwall a wide range of behaviour was tolerated, and that families who were always 'flashing the cash' were accepted as such. It was changing behaviour, trying to shift your position in society, that was frowned on.

Politeness was the most important ingredient of social intercourse. You greeted everyone with a 'Good Morning', and children would address adults as 'Mr' and 'Mrs', never by their first name. People hardly ever swore, certainly never 'in front of the ladies', and the use of bad language marked you down as someone of low birth. Bad manners were not tolerated and meant social exclusion. Generally, people met in the town, in church, in the various clubs and associations (like Mothers' Union) and in pubs. I recall very little socialising at home. 'An Englishman's home was his castle', and we knew very little about what went on behind closed doors. Although there is no doubt that some households were rife with abusive behaviour, I suspect that most were, like ours, generally happy. People generally respected each other's privacy, and we didn't really know much about our fellow citizens. Not that we didn't speculate because Looe was always awash with gossip, most of it juicy, slanderous and wildly inaccurate. Generally, though, England was a country of private, undemonstrative, reserved citizens for whom any kind of display was anathema.

So how did this rigid, orderly society loosen up to become the flamboyant entity it is today? Looking back on it, the device which changed our lives forever was the television set. It delivered exhibitionism into our front rooms, slowly at first, but with increasing confidence as the medium developed. Only people well over 60 now will remember life without the 'crystal bucket', as Clive James memorably dubbed it. We didn't have one when I was born, and I remember us all going to watch this new marvel in a neighbour's house. But we soon acquired one, and within ten years we were all hooked. I say ten years, because the early black and white TVs had dreadful reception, especially in Cornwall, and were not to be relied on as a source of entertainment. The real television era began in 1967, with the advent of colour TV, and it sucked us all in from then onwards. Its power, its ability to dominate one's life, is astonishing. In the 1950s, virtually every home had some form of religious imagery, like a crucifix or a picture of Jesus, and few had televisions. Now every home has at least one television, or device with a screen, and hardly any have a crucifix. It is a metaphor for modern life, the old religious symbols being replaced by a secular one.

Children naturally thought it was a brilliant invention but others were not so sure. In Cornwall it was referred to as the 'idiot box', not just for its content but because of the likely effect on its viewers. The older generation, who had grown up in a Cornwall still steeped in pagan lore, genuinely thought that it was the work of the devil.

Some church leaders and politicians shared the view that it had the potential to do great harm, both to the individual and society as a whole. A Warwickshire housewife, Mary White-house, set up the National Viewers and Listeners Association to monitor the quality of programmes, focusing especially on sex and bad language. She was widely ridiculed at the time, even having a pornographic magazine named after her, but 60 years on a lot of her concerns have become reality. Television is saturated with four letter words and sex, and the weird world of the small screen now seems to drive real life. In some cases it has replaced it. At seven o'clock in the evening there will be about two people in our local village pub, but within a mile radius at least 500 will be watching a soap opera which centres on ... the village pub. How odd is that?

It is also hardly possible to walk down a high street in Britain without hearing four letter words used as part of normal conversation. Years ago, people would have said something, but these days you are likely to get beaten up, or worse. You are also likely to see people aping some of the extravagant mannerisms of TV personalities as part of their normal conversation. The Britain I grew up in was quieter, but safer, and better mannered.

The early years of television were the golden years, remembered fondly by viewers and presenters alike. Perhaps our memories are tinged by the fact that there was actually very little to watch back in the sixties. There was the news and a children's programme at lunchtime, and then children's TV at five with programmes running through until eleven. For most of my childhood there were only two channels, BBC and ITV – BBC2 arrived in 1967, and Channel Four in 1982. No stations broadcast in the mornings or afternoons.

As it was a new media, the pioneers had to more or less make it up as they went along. I don't know why this leads to better quality, but it does, the lack of boundaries and templates meaning that the forerunners could create their own. The programmes tended to stick to generic headings, like drama, documentaries, current affairs, and light entertainment. The tone of most TV was serious, and there was no crossover between the various genres of programme. You would get exhibitionism in light entertainment, but that was expected, an echo of the old music hall.

Away from the small screen, the world was changing dramatically. In 1967 we saw the 'Summer of Love', the great hippie revolution which was meant to usher in the Age of Aquarius. It may not have ended war, or even given peace a chance, but it did see a revolution in personal exhibitionism. Men grew their hair long, and both sexes burst out of the narrow confines of dress and behaviour to wear multicoloured clothes and practice free love. Our parents were scandalised, even more so when the TV showed girls dancing topless at festivals. More seriously, 1968 saw a wave of civil unrest around the globe, with riots in Paris, and several US cities after the death of Martin Luther King. There were violent protests against the Vietnam war in most Western countries. It did seem as if the old order was being swept away.

One of the targets for the leaders of the revolution was the consumer society. The post-war technological and manufacturing boom saw a whole range of goods, like washing machines, fridges, and televisions, become affordable for the average family. People began to be defined by their possessions. Of these the most important was the car, the defining status symbol of the post war Western World. The car said something about you as a person because it was an exhibition of your taste and social position. The family man would drive a small saloon, a car bought for its practical value, the millionaire displaying his wealth with a Rolls Royce. The early petrolheads would go for a small sports car, the richer opting for a Jaguar, or an Aston Martin if you had a bit more class. When I was young even owning a car was a status symbol, until they began to be mass-produced in the fifties and sixties. Which led to another way of defining your status: the 'two-car' family. Car ownership was an early example of consumer exhibitionism because it was an unspoken demonstration of your personality. You may even be revealing something about yourself of which you are unaware. There are deep waters in consumerism, and monsters lurk in those depths.

One of them is the effect the car has on both our visible and invisible environment. Only very old people can now remember our towns and cities before the locust-like onslaught of the automobile. I mentioned in the previous chapter how our town centres were radically redeveloped in the 1950s and 1960s, and one of the prime movers behind that construction boom was the need to provide more roads and parking. I very much doubt whether any town in the country has been spared the construction of a new road, or that particular urban blight, the multi storey car park. If environmental ugliness counts as negative exhibitionism, then the car has been responsible for most of it. And that is before you get on to the effects of exhaust gases on the ozone layer, and the phenomenon of climate change.

Television made it possible for social attitudes to change by giving people a global audience. What happened in other countries was no longer remote but beamed directly into your living room. The revolution in music was made possible by technology – the invention of the transistor – and the modern industrial society's ability to mass-produce radios and television. What could have been local or national phenomena became global. A child at home in thirties Britain could listen to the radio or read the papers, but they were reliant on their family and community for both information and a social life. By the time it got to my generation, in the sixties, we were being overwhelmed by a completely alien culture, with radically different ideals and values. And our parents could not keep up. One of the lasting effects of this culture change and the rise of the new entertainment media was to drive a wedge between the generations.

Music was the defining art form of the new age. The soundtrack of the sixties was quite unlike anything else: fresh, innovative, and aimed straight at young people. The performers were completely different from previous musicians, dressing exotically and often behaving outrageously on stage. The Who and Jimi Hendrix smashed up their instruments at the end of a performance. Acts like Alice Cooper and Arthur Brown took it further, creating exhibitionist personalities which became part of the show. Alice Cooper pioneered gothic makeup and the use of stage sets, which included draping himself in a live python. (That particular experiment reached its nadir when Ozzy Osbourne bit the head off a live bat.)

The acts may have been outrageous, but they were still aggressively macho rock stars. A young South London singer/songwriter called David Bowie was about to change all that. He reinvented himself as Ziggy Stardust, a heavily made up, extravagantly dressed, androgynous, rock star, who was backed by the equally flamboyant Spiders from Mars. At a time when most rock acts dressed in jeans and T-shirt, Ziggy fused the world of music with the fashion industry, pioneering the highly visual, costume changing, act copied by so many of today's superstars. His deliberately androgynous appearance was also designed to be unsettling, especially when Bowie revealed that Ziggy was bisexual. By doing so he liberated a generation of young people to follow their instincts at a time when alternative sexuality was still actively persecuted. Others were not so sure – rock fans are essentially conservative, and quite a lot of us did not know what to make of Ziggy. As a result he never occupied the same place in people's affections as, say, the Beatles. And just as we were getting our head around it all, he announced, onstage, to widespread disbelief, that Ziggy Stardust and the Spiders From Mars were no more. Although bands were always splitting up and reforming, this was something quite different, an artist who deliberately killed off his most successful creation.

Bowie moved to the USA, where he experimented with funk and soul music, becoming one of the first white artists to appear on the variety show *Soul Train*. In the USA he developed his acting career in the film *The Man Who Fell to Earth*. Out of this came his next musical incarnation, The Thin White Duke, a Bowie take on a nightclub balladeer. The Thin White Duke had serious drug problems, developing a paranoia which led to a flirtation with fascism.

At this point Bowie's story could have followed the traditional rock star path to oblivion. Instead he moved back to Europe, kicked the drugs, and ended up in Berlin, exploring culture in its broadest sense. His next two albums, *Low* and *Heroes,* were synthesizer-based ambient music, widely panned at the time but since acclaimed as ground-breaking albums. He subsequently reinvented himself as an actor, whilst continuing to record, and tour, always remaining creatively restless. Each reincarnation was accompanied by a change of image, and each image was perfect for the persona he was trying to create. It is a measure of his success that the V&A Museum, the home of the decorative arts and design, is holding an exhibition of his costumes and memorabilia. He is, if you like, the exhibitionist's exhibitionist. And yet, who is David Bowie? Despite being the most flamboyant entertainer of his times, his continual reinvention has kept people guessing as to his true nature. Perhaps Bowie demonstrates that the best way to conceal your true self is to display many others.

David Bowie aside, it was the content of sixties music as much as anything else that set it apart from what had gone before. For a while it seemed that music was offering us a soundtrack for a whole new way of life, a rejection of society's obsession with money and possessions, offering a return to a simpler way of life. It is a matter of record that it never really happened. Instead, music rapidly became part of mainstream culture, and the performers zoomed up into the celebrity stratosphere. The Beatles became the most famous people on the planet, and had to be treated as such, separated from the real world by layers of managers and assistants. As the old hippies would have put it, 'the breadheads' took over. Far from signalling a return to simpler times, the musical revolution ushered in an era of rampant capitalism, and personal exhibitionism on the grand scale.

The process of that change was fascinating, particularly the development of that interesting creation, the media personality. It began on the radio, and was stimulated by the rise of the new music. In the early days the BBC would not broadcast 'pop' music, and the only way you could hear it was by listening to pirate radio stations like Radio Caroline. The main attraction was the music, but the DJs also became personalities in their own right, a very important milestone in the history of modern exhibitionism. In 1967 the BBC created Radio 1 as the pop music station, importing many of the old pirate radio DJs. Radio 1's first programme was the Tony Blackburn breakfast show, broadcast on 30 September 1967. Tony Blackburn had a unique style, mixing the music with a series of corny jokes and signature jingles, creating a brand which made him a celebrity. Other Radio 1 DJs followed suit, creating personalised programmes in which the music became almost secondary to the style of the show. This reached a peak with Steve Wright, who developed a cast of characters that resembled a mini soap opera. We listened to Steve Wright to hear the latest from 'Mr Angry from Purley', or 'Keef', a fantastic parody of the legendary Rolling Stone. The show became a work of art in itself, although such was its nature that at one handover a fellow DJ asked, only slightly ironically, 'any music on the show today?' The DJs were becoming famous for being famous, and although at their best, like Steve Wright, they were creative artists, they were still reliant on another product for their existence. The entertainment industry was beginning to offer careers for people whose main talent was for relentless self-promotion, the essential component of which was outrageous or exaggerated behaviour – pure exhibitionism.

This spread into television. Presenters achieved fame as 'TV personalities', and were drawn from all the specialities, not just light entertainment. News readers like Reggie Bosanquet, Anna Ford and Angela Rippon became stars, as did political interviewers like Robin Day, weathermen like Michael Fish, and chat show hosts, of which the best known was Michael

Parkinson. Although most of them had considerable experience in fields outside of the small screen, once they appeared
on TV they became part of that rarefied social strata, the world
of the celebrity. And this was not just driven by the personalities themselves, but by the public – we wanted to know more
about them, but we also needed to put them on a pedestal.

Even then they were few in number until the 1980s, when
two very important changes occurred. The first was the extension of broadcasting hours, which led to breakfast and afternoon TV, and ultimately 24-hour broadcasting. The second was
the licensing of satellite broadcasting, which not only created a
challenge to BBC and ITV, but also gave the public access to
over 100 other channels. The positive side of this revolution
was the chance it gave to broadcast minority or special interest
programmes, or to resurrect forgotten or previously unseen
material.

The downside was the need to fill all this airspace. There are,
after all, only so many comedy classics or soap operas to go
around. So, new types of programmes began to be created –
game shows, reality shows, cookery programmes, and all the
rest of the stuff that feeds the relentless appetite of 24-hour TV.
All these shows needed presenters, and from the late 1960s
onwards a recognisable type began to emerge – loud, extrovert,
quick-witted, and dressed extravagantly in shiny or spangled
suits. A good example of how it all began is Bob Monkhouse on
the ITV show *The Golden Shot*, and since then flamboyance has
been the by-word for the TV personality.

For the ordinary viewer this means that hardly a day will go
by without seeing some form of exhibitionist behaviour. You
are one click of the remote away from someone in a shiny
costume yabbering away at the camera. The ability to become
part of this celebrity culture becomes a goal in itself, so we are
bombarded with exhibitionist personalities elbowing their way
to the front of the screen.

And it is not just confined to the small screen. Footballers,
previously content to celebrate a goal with a manly handshake

and a trot back to the centre circle, are now more likely to rip their shirt off and flaunt their rippling torsos. Even more sedate sports have the 'look at me' fist pump to celebrate triumph. And the hinterland around sport is getting its fair share of rampant egotists as well – during the recent Olympics, it seemed as if some TV and radio presenters regarded the events as a backdrop for their personality, that in their minds they were at least as important as the athletes. This is relatively harmless in itself – you can always switch off when they're going on about what they had for breakfast – but there is a deeper problem. The evolution of television programmes, especially news and current affairs, has been subtle but profound. What began as a man in a dinner jacket simply reading out events became changed by the need to offer a different product from your rivals. The structure of news programmes became stratified, and began to include the folksy little item at the end. And newsreaders and reporters developed a following. Broadcast journalists went from being straight reporters, to recognisable faces, to personalities, to personalities who tinge their reports with subjective language.

This form of exhibitionism has had two very important, and dangerous, effects. Somewhere along the line, the art of objective reporting got diluted. George Orwell wrote that prose should be like a pane of glass: that the reader should be able to understand clearly what was being said. It was the journalist's job to reveal the truth, however unpalatable that may be to them personally, and for a long time that held true. Now it is almost impossible to see a news item without the personality of the presenter intervening.

Before the television age, politicians would go out 'on the stump', holding public meetings to discuss their policies. It would be quite possible for an ordinary member of the public to meet a noted politician. Now it is all done through the media, and anyone wishing to become Prime Minister has to conform to their rules, both in terms of the tone of debate and in their ability to handle the self-regarding inquisitors of the

TV and newspapers. The values the public might like in a politician (honesty, reliability, the ability to understand complex organisations like the NHS) are irrelevant to this process. What matters is the politician's ability to negotiate the shark infested waters of the media – a political complex known as the Westminster Village. The exhibitionist media culture of the twenty-first century also demands a series of vivid soundbites which can be recycled to dramatise future programmes. At its worst a political interview consists of a media personality trying to get a damning admission out of an eminent politician, who is equally determined not to answer. Frequently this focuses on personalities, who said what to whom, rather than the deeper underlying questions. The most notable example of this was Jeremy Paxman's 1997 *Newsnight* interview with the Conservative politician Michael Howard, when Paxman asked the same question twelve times without receiving a satisfactory reply. (The interview can be seen on YouTube; see the references section at the back of this book.) We can even become complicit in the process, hoping that Jeremy Paxman or John Humphrys provide us with some fireworks. This may be an inevitable consequence of our growing political sophistication, and the fading of deference, but there are dangers. When I was old enough to vote, in 1971, Westminster contained a large proportion of MPs who had tangible experience of the real world before becoming an MP. Frequently they had a network of connections and roots in the constituencies they represented. They were not television material, though, often being overweight, slightly scruffy, and relatively physically unattractive men and women. Although that type of MP has not disappeared, the successful modern MP is more likely to be a professional politician, toned and well groomed, someone who understands the path to power. (To understand the difference, compare photographs of Harold Wilson and Edward Heath, Labour and Conservative leaders in the seventies, with Tony Blair and David Cameron.) The problem with this is the gap which has opened up between ordinary folk and the political process, and the danger is that ordinary people will begin to see politics as irrelevant. To give you an example, I worked in the NHS for 30 years. What the NHS needs is a period of stability, a chance to rediscover the team spirit and sense of community which were the features of my early years in the service. Instead, it gets precisely the opposite, being reorganised by every incoming government. As one student union, sorry, government, gets replaced by another you begin to wonder – why am I voting for this? What do these people know about running a huge, complex, healthcare system? Self-promotion and lust for power are one thing, competence and intellect quite another. Exhibitionism is the path to power, and it could be destroying us.

So, in the space of 50 years, a blink of an eye in human history, the story of exhibitionism has changed. The closed-in, private society where showing off was frowned upon has become one where public display is looked on with approval. And exhibitionism, the ability to behave extravagantly, can be rewarded with fame and success in the world of celebrity. This has been made possible by the technological society, the mush-rooming of television, and the change in society's values which distilled off from the social revolution of the sixties.

It is an interesting coincidence that the rise in human exhibitionism has seen the science of psychology move from its origins with Freud and Jung to the complex discipline that it is today. Although we are all aware of how psychology works in everyday life because we instinctively judge the way people behave, we are perhaps less aware of the way psychological techniques are used to influence our behaviour. Advertising, in particular, has long been aware of the best methods to attract our attention, using dramatic images, repetition and humour to hook us on to a product. Every time we see an advert on the TV we are being conditioned by this process. The most important goal for a manufacturer is to get a product recognised as a brand, with a distinctive and unique identity. The recent Olympics in London were a good example of this, with only licensed brands like McDonald's and Coca-Cola sold in the Olympic complex. Corporate exhibitionism is a very important development of the modern era, as the rise of the global brand testifies. We may think that it is all a bit of a joke, but we all cherish a favourite somewhere, be it Coca-Cola, Marlboro, Budweiser, Rolex, or whatever. This also applies to stores and shop chains like Marks and Spencer, Boots, and Starbucks. The old surrealists would surely have appreciated the way that these 'branded' shops have made everywhere look like everywhere else. And in the worlds of sport and entertainment exactly the same thing is happening. Famous sportsmen become 'brands', like Tiger Woods and Roger Federer. So do entertainers like Stephen Fry and Russell, er, Brand. And in the same way that the branded multinationals are way above the poor small businessmen, so these branded celebrities inhabit a world almost completely removed from ordinary life.

If psychology has helped the commercial world, it has also helped us define the exhibitionist by sorting the various examples of extreme human behaviour into personality disorders. The best fit for the compulsive celebrity/presenter exhibitionist is the 'histrionic' personality disorder, whose features can be remembered by the mnemonic 'PRAISE ME':

> **P**rovocative (or seductive) behaviour
> **R**elationships considered more intimate than they
>   actually are
> **A**ttention seeking
> **I**nfluenced easily
> **S**peech designed to impress, lacking detail
> **E**motional ability, shallowness
> **M**ake up – attention-seeking physical appearance
> **E**xaggerated emotions and theatrical behaviour

Anyone who has followed the careers of the rich and famous will recognise those characteristics. In general, though, the actions of the exhibitionist performer are designed to catch your attention in a favourable way. Sometimes the worship of self becomes unhealthy, and tips over into a 'narcissistic' personality disorder, or megalomania, as it used to be known. This has some disturbing features:

- Difficulty accepting criticism
- Taking advantage of others to achieve their aims
- Requiring constant attention and positive reinforcement
- Exaggerating their own importance
- Wanting the best of everything
- Fantasising about achievements
- Emotionally sterile

I would suggest that the biographies of some famous people reveal these traits in abundance. In the modern world it seems that not only do celebrities feel free to behave differently from the rest of us, but they are actually encouraged to do so, and in many cases are actually trapped into a personality from which they can't escape. An example was the writer Evelyn Waugh, who created an acerbic, rude, and prickly public persona that obscured his personal warmth, brilliant conversation, and many acts of kindness. His biographer Selina Hastings, and his friend Nancy Mitford, believed that he had invented the 'Crusty Colonel' persona as a joke, but found himself overwhelmed by his creation. Show business abounds, too, with tales of apparently warm hearted, matey personalities, who are the complete opposite in real life. At the time of writing one of Britain's 'national treasures', the late Jimmy Savile, has been exposed as a predatory paedophile whose offences date back 40 years.

We expect extravagant behaviour from our celebrities and media creations. But what of ourselves? Do we really wish the same degree of exposure for our private lives? Has society really changed that much in the last 50 years? The answer is that it has, and just as television changed the world of celebrity exhibitionism for ever, so the personal computer has changed the world of individual exhibitionism.

Before the advent of the personal computer, you would only be known by people you met face-to-face, or corresponded with by phone or letter. The number of people you knew would depend on your personality and your employment, but for most people I would guess that this would number at most about 100. To become known to more people, you would probably have to have achieved fame in some form of media or artistic capacity, which meant demonstrating unusual talent or ability. The vast majority of the population therefore remained unknown outside of their social or employment circles. People knew as much about you as you chose to reveal. Activities like shopping were a simple transaction between you and the retailer, and quickly forgotten by both parties. There was no lasting record, you were not being targeted or profiled. You could fall around drunk in a town centre without being captured on CCTV, and if you went out for the day nobody would know where you were. In a closed world much of what you did remained unknown. Paradoxically, when you did venture forth, your personal standing depended on how you reacted with other people. You don't tend to upset those who you are likely to see for the next 50 years, your behaviour is modified by your circumstances.

The personal computer changed all that by giving the user a whole new world to contact. Although computers date from the 1950s, personal computers only became available in the 1970s, and their rise has been phenomenal. In 1977, 48,000 PCs had been produced, by 2002 this had risen to over one billion. The internet was invented by Tim Berners-Lee back in 1980, and had evolved to carry personal and commercial traffic by the 1990s. Initially you needed to be techno-savvy to create your own content, but from the late 1990s onwards increasingly sophisticated software meant that non-technical users could post content online. Blogging, creating 'web-logs' of personal or corporate content began around this time. Email, sending text messages electronically actually owed its origins to morse code, but became user friendly in the 1980s with the advent of the PC. The effect of these developments is to revolutionise the individual's ability to shop, to find out information, and to interact with others online.

It is hard to overestimate how important these changes have been, and how fast the world is changing. Thirty years ago, if I had wanted a record or a book I'd have had to travel to get one. Much as I vowed to keep in touch with old friends, I never got round to writing the letter, or making the phone call, until email made contact so much easier. And for the researcher, the internet has revolutionised access to information. You can do in a morning what it would have taken weeks to achieve just a short time ago.

As the various functions of the internet became more sophisticated it was clear that it had evolved way beyond its original format. The term 'Web 2.0' was coined to describe the new entity, entering general use back in 2002. The key difference was the power it gave to the individual user to share information, co-operate, and generate one's own content. The possibility of an online virtual community was now reality. More impressively, online monitoring services can profile your usage, and tailor advertisements and product information to match your tastes.

Facebook was invented in 2004, and Twitter began in 2006. These interactive social media are redefining both social interaction and one's personal profile. Facebook was enthusiastically embraced by the computer generation, especially the young, and it spread like wildfire. The content of some sites was uninhibited, with uncensored pictures and text, creating a whole new generation of exhibitionists. And like all things, the dark side soon became apparent, with bullying, 'unfriending', and the creation of false identities by the unscrupulous to prey on the vulnerable.

Not that many people have gone this far. At the time of writing, Facebook appears to have peaked, and the early rush of users, which saw some spectacular postings of individual excess, seemed to have settled down. In many ways it has replaced the telephone as a social organiser, enabling friends to keep in touch and arrange meetings. It is also a great way to share experiences relatively painlessly. (Veterans of seventies and eighties dinner party circuits will remember the, 'and this is us in Benidorm' moments, as yet another brick of holiday snaps landed on the table.)

The positive side of being able to post content online is the ability of individuals to conduct business, express opinions and advertise themselves, or their projects. The ease with which we can use the net means that the number of transactions has increased exponentially. Even the most avid letter writer could probably only manage a couple a day, say five or six hundred a year, whereas it is certainly possible to send a hundred emails in a week. And to get an opinion into the public domain is made easy by the response columns to online content. No more waiting to see if the newspaper has published your letter, it is there at the click of a button.

Anyone who was fortunate to get a letter published in the national press was aware of the 'green ink' writers, the people who would send vicious and abusive responses to your opinions in a variety of coloured inks. Newspaper columnists and other public figures were well aware of this phenomenon, which was fortunately rare due to the time it took to compose a letter, and post it.

Alas, this is no more, because the new technology enables these people to adopt a scattergun approach to vitriolic abuse. Some of it is banter, and some just plain barmy, but much of it is nasty, vicious and personal. The internet 'trolls' who indulge in this are taking advantage of the anonymity of the web to say things they would never get away with in real life. Much of it is directed at celebrity bloggers and tweeters, many of whom have had to disconnect from social media to escape persecution. When Jeremy Clarkson, the *Top Gear* presenter, announced on Twitter that his dog had died, the responses that he received caused him to brand Britain as a nation of '62 million utter bastards'. Stephen Fry, a 'twittionaire' with five million followers, observed of some trolls that 'their resentment, their desire to be heard at the most unpleasant and malevolent, genuinely ill-willed malevolent level is terrifying.' The flat stone has been lifted up and all sorts of creatures are crawling out.

Not that the vast majority of users are exhibiting an extravagantly unpleasant personality. But we are exhibiting ourselves, however innocuously. Every time we log onto an internet site, we create a record, and are building up a picture of our tastes, and ultimately ourselves. This is fraught with difficulty, because the picture we present to the world through computer usage is ultimately a distorted one.

Or is it? I suspect that if we wrote down a day's worth of activities, and then wrote down what we did on the computer, then we would get a pretty good match. If I think about it, virtually every part of my life creates a record somewhere. From reading a newspaper (subscriber) to shopping at Tesco or buying books from a bookshop, with a loyalty card, most things leave a trail. I can be traced even walking the dog, because the dog has got an electronic tag, and if I take my mobile phone then so have I. It is quite frightening if you think about it; more than frightening, according to the British technology writer A. J. Keen. He likens the modern internet to the philosopher Jeremy Bentham's 'Panopticon' – a building which enabled a central watchman to observe all the activities of the inhabitants, who may not have been aware that they were being observed. The most obvious application of the design was in the building of prisons, and several, like Port Arthur in Tasmania, were constructed along these lines.

The parallels with personal computer use are disturbing. Regular users of the web are leaving a trail by downloading 'cookies', links to specific sites which remain on your computer. Mostly they are sites that you have visited, and may contain your log-in details if it is a protected site. Most are generated by the user. There are, however, cookies attached to banner advertisements that contain links to sites you may not visit. All these cookies can be detected, and used to profile your internet use. Anyone wishing to know your preferences find out by targeting your computer, be they government agencies, or commercial organisations. You may even just be part of a general sweep by a profiling agency. This is a simplification of a complex process, but the message is that once you get into the system it is hard to escape. Once your browser gets to work, the lights go on all over the internet.

You have now become two people. One is the 'me' who inhabits your body and moves through life in real time. The second is your online persona, whose threads can be traced back to you, but who does other things apart from buying wine or books from Amazon. In real life I value my privacy, but my online 'me' is on display all the time. And is it me? How much of my personal information is simply inaccurate? Out there I am known as Chris Nanwollas, Dame C. Nancollas, Chris Nancholas, cnanc, and Chris Nancolleth, among others. Do we each have a cell in the virtual Panopticon, I wonder?

Andrew Keen's latest book is called *Digital Vertigo,* a nod to the Hitchcock film in which a man falls in love with a woman pretending to be someone else. The creation of virtual persona, and identity theft, is now frighteningly simple for the techno-savvy. One of the central arguments of *Digital Vertigo* is that the web, which we all saw as a tool for personal enrichment, has now evolved into a typical human hierarchy. Our lives are dominated, and controlled, by the new Masters of the Virtual Universe, a world which is exclusive because of its complexity. Power is residing in the controllers of the networks, the 'Super Nodes' in technospeak, and some of the operators see personal privacy as an out-dated concept. Censorship has become impossible, and morality an historical curiosity. Keen, who has dubbed himself 'the Antichrist of Silicon Valley' thinks the process is dehumanising us, undermining centuries of human progress.

He is particularly scathing about the way technology allows each of us to write a blog, make a film, or record a song, and then post the results online. The result is a net stuffed full of amateur talent, most of which is of no artistic value whatsoever. Keen thinks that this 'digital narcissism' is dangerous, encouraging an overinflated view of the self that is psychologically harmful. He also believes that file sharing and free music downloads will conspire with the assault on traditional publishing to kill off the music and publishing industries. The genuinely talented exhibitionist performer has been joined by hundreds of thousands of wannabes. Not just in the field of the arts, either, there are thousands of official looking websites offering things like health advice which are bordering on dangerous. The internet is fertile ground for the modern snake-oil salesman, purveyors of quack remedies and mythical cures.

Where all this will end up is anybody's guess. Andy Warhol said in 1968, that 'in the future, everyone will be famous for fifteen minutes'. This is widely invoked as 'fifteen minutes of fame', usually when a previously unknown performer achieves success in an artistic or sporting field. But Warhol, the great deconstructor of art, was looking at something more profound, the deconstruction of fame itself. To be famous, we need to exhibit ourselves, and we now have the means to do it. Centuries of painstaking advances in the elitist worlds of art, literature, and entertainment have suddenly been violently democratised. Even the flasher in a public park finds himself competing with a cast of thousands on the internet. When everybody is on display all of the time, who then are the exhibitionists? That is the question the 21st century has to answer.

Bibliography

The titles of useful background reading are in the order that the subject matter appears in the book. I have named the edition of the reference books that I used, which may not be the most recent.

Chapter 1: Introduction and Chapter 2: The history of exhibitionism

The Man Who Went Into the West: The Life of R. S. Thomas by Byron Rogers (Aurum, 2006).
ISBN 978-1-84513-250-7

The History of the World by J. M. Roberts (Pelican Books, 1980).
ISBN 987-0-141-90089-6

Stonehenge by Rosemary Hill (Profile Books, 2008).
ISBN 978-1-86197-865-3

Rumpole of the Bailey by John Mortimer (Penguin, 1978).
ISBN 978–0140046700

The Oxford History of the Classical World (OUP, 1986).
ISBN 978-0-198-72112-3

Greek Myths by Robert Graves (Penguin, 1991).
ISBN 978-0-140-17199-0

Rome by Robert Hughes (Weidenfeld and Nicolson, 2011).
ISBN 978-0-297-84464-8

The Oxford History of Christianity (OUP, 1990).
ISBN 0-19-822928-3

Islam by Karen Armstrong (Phoenix, 2001).
ISBN 978-1-842-12583-0

Buddhism Plain and Simple by Steve Hagen (Penguin, 1997).
ISBN 978-0-140-195965-5

Images of Lust by Anthony Weir and James Jerman (Batsford Books, 1986).
ISBN 0-7134-5110-6

Cambridge Illustrated History of The Middle Ages (Press syndicate of the University of Cambridge, 3 volume set).
ISBN 0-521-59078-7

Gloucester Cathedral (Scala Books, 2011).
ISBN 978-1-85759-667-0

A History of Britain by Simon Schama (BBC Books, 2000).
ISBN 0-563-38497-2

Exhibitionism by Brett Kahr, *Ideas in Psychoanalysis* series (Icon Books, 2001).
ISBN 1-84046-275-2

Foundation by Peter Ackroyd (Macmillan 2011).
ISBN 978-0-230-70632-2

History of Psychiatry by Edward Shorter (John Wiley & Sons, 1997).
ISBN 0-471-15749-X

Chapter 3: Sexual exhibitionism

Most of the medical and psychological content of this chapter is taken from two books:

Exhibitionism by Brett Kahr (see above) and Sexual *Deviance, Theory, Assessment and Treatment* by Laws and O'Donahue (second edition, Guildford Press, 2008).
ISBN 978–1593856052

Images of Lust by Anthony Weir and James Jerman (Batsford Books, 1986).
ISBN 0-7134-5110-6

Terry Jones's Medieval Lives by Terry Jones and Alan Ereira (BBC Books, 2005).
ISBN 978–0563522751

To Althea, From Prison by Richard Lovelace 1649, *The Oxford Book of English Verse*, Sir Arthur Quiller-Couch (ed.) (OUP, 1900).

American Psychiatric Association, *DSM-IV, the Diagnostic and Statistical Manual of Mental Disorders* APA, 1994.
ISBN 978–0890420256

Sexual Deviance, Theory, Assessment, and Treatment, Richard D. Laws and William T. O'Donohue (eds.).

The Essentials of Psychoanalysis by Sigmund Freud (Pelican Books, 1986).
ISBN 0-14-022683-4

Exhibitionism and Other Sex Aberrations by Alex Legray (Diamond Star Books, 1969).

The Female Eunuch by Germaine Greer (Harper Perennial, 2006; first published 1970).
ISBN 978-0-00-720501-1

An English Affair by Richard Davenport-Hines (Harper, 2012).
ISBN 978–0007435845

Chapter 4: Exhibitionism as public display 1: representational art

The $12 Million Stuffed Shark: The Curious Economics of Contemporary Art and Auction Houses by Don Thomson (Aurum, 2008).
ISBN 978-1-84513-302-3

Egypt Revealed by T. G. H. James (Folio Society, 1997).

Art – The Whole Story by Stephen Farthing (ed.) (Thames and Hudson, 2010).
ISBN 978-0-500-28895-5

The Story of Art by E. H. Gombrich (Phaidon Books, 2006, pocket edition).
ISBN 978-0-7148-4703-0

Dada and Surrealism: A Very Short Introduction by David Hopkins (Oxford University Press, 2004).
ISBN 978-0-19-280254-5

Surrealism by Catherin Klinsohr-Leroy, ed. Uta Grosenick (Taschen Books, 2011).
ISBN978-3-8365-1419-4

The Painted Word by Tom Wolfe (Picador USA, 2008).
ISBN 978–0312427580

Discovering the Present: Three Decades in Art, Culture and Politics by Harold Rosenburg (University of Chicago Press, 1973).
ISBN 0-226-72680-0

Exhibitionism by Lynne Munson (Ivan R. Dee, 2000).
ISBN 1-56663-399-0

Chapter 5: Exhibitionism as public display 2: the performing arts

The Ordinalia: The Cornish Mystery Play Cycle by Alan M. Kent (Francis Boutle, 2006).
ISBN 987–1903427279

Oxford Companion to English Literature, Margaret Drabble (ed.) (OUP, 1985).
ISBN 0-19-866130-4

Two Dissertations on the Theatre by Theophilius Cibber, 1756 (Lightning Source, 2011).
ISBN 978–1235799396

A Mencken Chrestomathy by H. L. Mencken (Vintage Books, 1982).
ISBN 978–0394752099

The Essential Jung, Anthony Storr (ed.) (Fontana Press, 1983).
ISBN 0-00-653065-6

Psychological Reflections by C. G. Jung (Ark Paperbacks, 1971).
ISBN 0-7448-0036-6

Introduction to Type by Isabel Briggs Myers (Oxford Psychologists Press, 1993).
ISBN 1-85639-060-8

Please Understand Me: Character And Temperament Types by David Keirsey and Marilyn Bates (Prometheus Nemesis Book Co., 1984).
ISBN 978–0960695409

The Actor, Image, and Action, Acting and Cognitive Neuroscience by Rhoda Blair (Routledge, 2008).
ISBN 978-0-415-77417-8

Waiting for Godot by Samuel Beckett. (Faber and Faber, 2006). ISBN 978–0571229116

When the Wind Changed: The Life and Death of Tony Hancock (Century 1999). ISBN 0-7126-7615-5

Tommy Cooper by John Fisher (Harper, 2006). ISBN 978-0-00-721511-9

Billy by Pamela Stephenson (HarperCollins, 2001). ISBN 0-00-711091-X

Spike by Norma Farnes (Harper Perennial, 2004). ISBN 1-84115-787-2

Puckoon by Spike Milligan (Penguin, 1973). ISBN 978–0140023749

Adolf Hitler: My Part in His Downfall by Spike Milligan (Penguin, 1986). 978–0140035209

Chapter 6: Exhibitionism and power

Britain A.D. by Francis Prior (HarperPerennial, 2005). ISBN 978–007181872

Stonehenge by Rosemary Hill (see above).

Travels in the History Of Architecture by Robert Harbison (Reaktion Books, 2011). ISBN 978–1861898180

The Great Pyramid Revisited by John Romer (Cambridge University Press, 2001). ISBN 978-0-521-69053-9

Supernature by Lyall Watson (Coronet Books, 1974). ISBN 978–0340188330

The Legacy of Greece, R.W. Livingstone (ed.) (Oxford University Press, 1921).

Oxford History of the Classical World (see above).

Rome by Robert Hughes (see above).

Gloucester Cathedral (see above).

Oxford History Of Britain, Kenneth O. Morgan (ed.) (OUP, 1988).
ISBN 978-0-192852021

A History of Britain by Simon Schama (see above).

Oxford Dictionary of Architecture by James Stevens Curl (OUP, 2006).
ISBN 978-0-19-860678-9

Museums without Walls by Jonathan Meades (Unbound Books, 2012).
ISBN 9781908717184

Autobiography of An Unknown Indian by Nirad Chaudhuri (Jaico Books, 2004).
ISBN 978–8172242879

Burmese Days by George Orwell (Penguin Classics, 2001).
ISBN 987–0141185378

Flashman And The Dragon by George Macdonald Fraser (William Collins Sons and Co., 1985).
ISBN 0-00-271245-8

Chapter 7: Exhibitionism in the modern world

Philip Larkin: Collected Poems (Faber and Faber, 1988).
ISBN 978–0571151967

Family Britain by David Kynaston (Bloomsbury, 2010).
ISBN 978–140880836

The Crystal Bucket by Clive James (Picador, 1983).
ISBN 0330267450

The Sixties by Jenny Diski (Profile Books, 2009).
ISBN 978-1-84668-003-6

1968: The Year That Rocked The World by Mark Kurlansky (Vintage Books, 2005).
ISBN 978–0099429623

Shout: The True Story Of The Beatles by Philip Norman (Pan, 2004).
ISBN 978–0283073330

The Lives of John Lennon by Albert Goldman (Bantam Press, 1988).
ISBN 978–0593015476

Why I Write by George Orwell (Penguin, first published 1946).
ISBN 978–0141019000

A First Course in Psychology by Nicky Hayes (Nelson, 1984).
ISBN 978–0174481812

ICD-10 Classification of Mental and Behavioural Disorders (World
Health Organisation, 1992).
ISBN 978–9241544221

Diagnostic and Statistical Manual of Mental Disorders, DSM-IV,
American Psychiatric Association (see above).

Evelyn Waugh by Selina Hastings (Sinclair Stevenson, 1994).
ISBN 978–1856192231

David Bowie, The Definitive Biography by Paul Trynka (Sphere,
2012).
ISBN 978–0751542936

Digital Vertigo by A. J. Keen (Constable, 2012).
ISBN 978–1780338408

Index

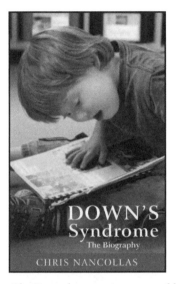

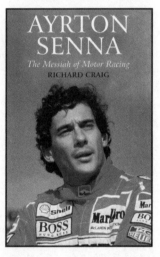